Applied Natural Language Processing with PyTorch 2.0

Master Advanced NLP Techniques, Transform Text Data into Insights, and Build Scalable AI Models with PyTorch 2.0

Dr. Deepti Chopra

www.orangeava.com

First Published: January 2025

Published By: Orange Education Pvt Ltd, AVA®

Address: 9, Daryaganj, Delhi, 110002, India

275 New North Road Islington Suite 1314 London,
N1 7AA, United Kingdom

ISBN (PBK): 978-93-48107-15-2
ISBN (E-BOOK): 978-93-48107-52-7

Scan the QR code to explore our entire catalogue

www.orangeava.com

Dedicated To

My Family

and

Friends

About the Author

Dr. Deepti Chopra is an accomplished academician at the School of Engineering & Technology, Vivekananda Institute of Professional Studies, India, specializing in Information Technology with a primary focus on Natural Language Processing (NLP) and Artificial Intelligence (AI). With over 11 years of experience in academia, she has made significant contributions to both research and teaching. Dr. Chopra's expertise includes Machine Translation, Named Entity Recognition, Morphological Analysis, and Machine Transliteration.

Deepti began her academic journey by obtaining a Bachelor's degree in Computer Science and Engineering from Rajasthan College of Engineering for Women. Throughout her undergraduate studies, she consistently excelled and secured top positions in her college. Driven by her passion for language and technology, she pursued a Master's degree in Computer Science and Engineering from Banasthali Vidyapith, where she once again showcased exceptional skills and graduated with top honors.

Motivated to delve deeper into her research interests, Deepti pursued a Ph.D. in Computer Science and Engineering from Banasthali Vidyapith. Her doctoral research revolved around enhancing the quality of Machine Translation, and she achieved remarkable success in this area. Consequently, she earned a Ph.D. degree with a specialization in Quality Improvement of Machine Translation. Her doctoral work resulted in the publication of numerous research papers and the granting of an Australian patent for her innovative approach to Named Entity Translation.

Deepti's commitment to advancing knowledge in her field is reflected in her extensive publication record. She has authored multiple books such as *Building Machine Learning Systems using Python* and *Flutter and Dart: Up and Running*. Additionally, her research papers have been published in reputable international conferences and journals.

Deepti's commitment and her ability to translate research findings into practical solutions solidify her position as a prominent figure in the field.

About the Technical Reviewer

Aniruddha Bhattacharjee is an accomplished professional with over 11 years of experience in designing and engineering data-intensive enterprise applications, deployed both on-premises and in the cloud. His expertise spans industries such as telecommunications, finance, and manufacturing.

Throughout his career, Aniruddha has collaborated with renowned organizations, including Ericsson, TCS, and Tavant Technologies, contributing to R&D and providing technical consultancy. Currently serving as a **Senior Data Scientist** at Tavant Technologies, he empowers global clients by delivering reliable and scalable data science solutions. In order to solve difficult business problems, he focuses on advancing digital transformation by integrating AI and GenAI technologies.

Aniruddha is deeply committed to leading data-driven initiatives that help organizations embrace cutting-edge technologies, improve operational efficiency, accelerate growth, and enhance decision-making. Beyond client engagements, he has played a key role in developing AI products, designing innovative, scalable, and impactful solutions across various sectors.

A passionate mentor and team builder, Aniruddha takes pride in nurturing expert teams that drive successful transformations. He fosters collaborative environments that encourage innovation, enabling sustainable business success.

In addition to his technical contributions, Aniruddha has served as a **technical reviewer**, offering valuable insights to ensure the quality and relevance of advancements in AI and data science. Dedicated to expanding the frontiers of AI and data technologies, he continues to make a profound impact across industries.

Acknowledgements

Writing this book has been a journey that would not have been possible without the support and guidance of many individuals. I am deeply grateful to each one of them. First and foremost, I would like to thank my family for their unwavering support and encouragement throughout this process. Your faith in my abilities gave me the confidence to see this project through to completion. To my editor and publishing team at Orange AVA, thank you for your expertise, patience, and dedication. Their insights and guidance have been invaluable in shaping this book into what it is today. A heartfelt thanks to my readers; this book was written with you in mind. Thank you for sharing in this journey with me.

Preface

This book on *Applied Natural Language Processing with PyTorch 2.0* is a comprehensive resource for data scientists, machine learning engineers, NLP practitioners, researchers, academics, software engineers, data analysts, linguists, and AI enthusiasts. It covers the latest advancements in PyTorch 2.0 for building cutting-edge NLP models and solutions. The book provides theoretical foundations, practical implementation guidance, and hands-on examples, making it suitable for both experienced practitioners and newcomers in the field of NLP. Whether you want to extend your PyTorch expertise to NLP, stay updated with the latest techniques, or explore deep learning for text analysis, this book has you covered.

This book is divided into 10 chapters. They will cover NLP topics and its implementation in Pytorch 2.0. The details are listed as follows:

Chapter 1. discusses an Introduction to Natural Language Processing (NLP). The topics covered in this chapter are about NLP, its applications, and various Challenges and Approaches in NLP.

Chapter 2. discusses about PyTorch 2.0. Various topics covered in this chapter are introduction to PyTorch 2.0, Installation of PyTorch 2.0, PyTorch Basics, Tensors and Operations and GPU Acceleration with PyTorch.

Chapter 3. discusses Text Preprocessing. Various topics covered include Tokenization, Stop Word Removal, Stemming and Lemmatization, Handling Special Characters and Punctuation, Word Embeddings and Word2Vec.

Chapter 4. discusses Building NLP Models with PyTorch. This chapter covers Text Classification, Sentiment Analysis, Named Entity Recognition (NER), Part-of-Speech (POS) Tagging, Machine Translation, and Text Generation with Recurrent Neural Networks (RNNs)

Chapter 5. discusses Advanced znLP Techniques with PyTorch. This chapter covers Sequence-to-Sequence Models, Attention Mechanisms, Transformer Models,T ransfer Learning for NLP and Language Modeling with GPT-3.5

Chapter 6. discusses Model Training and Evaluation. This chapter covers Dataset Preparation, Training Pipelines, Model Evaluation Metrics, Hyperparameter Tuning, Overfitting and Regularization Techniques.

Chapter 7. discusses Improving NLP Models with PyTorch 2.0. This chapter covers Handling Out-of-Vocabulary (OOV) Words, Handling Long Sequences, Batch Processing and Data Loaders, Advanced Optimization Techniques, Model Interpretability, and Explainability.

Chapter 8. discusses Deployment and Productionization. This chapter discusses about Exporting PyTorch Models, Deployment Strategies (Server, Edge, Cloud), Scaling and Performance Optimization, Monitoring and Debugging, and Ethical Considerations in NLP.

Chapter 9. discusses Case Studies and Practical Examples. This chapter discusses Sentiment Analysis on Social Media Data, Text Classification for News Articles, Chatbot Development with PyTorch, Neural Machine Translation System, and Question Answering Systems.

Chapter 10. discusses Future Trends in NLP and PyTorch. This chapter discusses Advances in Pretrained Language Models, Multilingual NLP and Cross-Lingual Transfer Learning, Explainable AI in NLP, Integration of NLP with Computer Vision, and Reinforcement Learning for NLP.

Get a Free eBook

We hope you are enjoying your recently purchased book! Your feedback is incredibly valuable to us, and to all other readers looking for great books.

If you found this book helpful or enjoyable, we would truly appreciate it, if you could take a moment to leave a short review with a 5 star rating on Amazon. It helps us grow, and lets other readers discover our books.

As a thank you, we would love to send you a free digital copy of this book, and a **30%** discount code on your next cart value on our official websites:

www.orangeava.com

www.orangeava.in (For Indian Subcontinent)

☑ **Here's how:**

Leave a review for the book on Amazon.

Take a screenshot of your review, and send an email to **info@orangeava.com** (it can be just the confirmation screen).

Once, we receive your screenshot, we will send you the digital file, within 24 hours.

Thank you so much for your support – it means a lot to us!

Downloading the code bundles and colored images

Please follow the links or scan the QR codes to download the ***Code Bundles and Images*** of the book:

https://github.com/ava-orange-education/Applied-Natural-Language-Processing-with-PyTorch-2.0

The code bundles and images of the book are also hosted on ***https://rebrand.ly/fd3176***

In case there's an update to the code, it will be updated on the existing GitHub repository.

Errata

We take immense pride in our work at **Orange Education Pvt Ltd,** and follow best practices to ensure the accuracy of our content to provide an indulging reading experience to our subscribers. Our readers are our mirrors, and we use their inputs to reflect and improve upon human errors, if any, that may have occurred during the publishing processes involved. To let us maintain the quality and help us reach out to any readers who might be having difficulties due to any unforeseen errors, please write to us at :

errata@orangeava.com

Your support, suggestions, and feedback are highly appreciated.

DID YOU KNOW

Did you know that Orange Education Pvt Ltd offers eBook versions of every book published, with PDF and ePub files available? You can upgrade to the eBook version at **www.orangeava.com** and as a print book customer, you are entitled to a discount on the eBook copy. Get in touch with us at: **info@orangeava.com** for more details.

At **www.orangeava.com**, you can also read a collection of free technical articles, sign up for a range of free newsletters, and receive exclusive discounts and offers on AVA® Books and eBooks.

PIRACY

If you come across any illegal copies of our works in any form on the internet, we would be grateful if you would provide us with the location address or website name. Please contact us at **info@orangeava.com** with a link to the material.

ARE YOU INTERESTED IN AUTHORING WITH US?

If there is a topic that you have expertise in, and you are interested in either writing or contributing to a book, please write to us at **business@orangeava.com**. We are on a journey to help developers and tech professionals to gain insights on the present technological advancements and innovations happening across the globe and build a community that believes Knowledge is best acquired by sharing and learning with others. Please reach out to us to learn what our audience demands and how you can be part of this educational reform. We also welcome ideas from tech experts and help them build learning and development content for their domains.

REVIEWS

Please leave a review. Once you have read and used this book, why not leave a review on the site that you purchased it from? Potential readers can then see and use your unbiased opinion to make purchase decisions. We at Orange Education would love to know what you think about our products, and our authors can learn from your feedback. Thank you!

For more information about Orange Education, please visit **www.orangeava.com**.

Table of Contents

Chapter 1
Introduction to Natural Language Processing

Introduction

Nowadays, there has been an increase in data as well as technological innovation. This has been due to advancements in Natural Language Processing (NLP), which have bridged the gap between human language and technology, making it easier to interpret, comprehend, and communicate information in the world. NLP has improved the way humans interact with technology and among each other. This chapter, *Introduction to Natural Language Processing*, is a base for our journey of NLP, where we will unravel its intricacies, explore its applications, and delve deeper into the challenges as well as innovative approaches that define this dynamic field.

Natural Language Processing, often abbreviated as NLP, is the interdisciplinary field comprising areas such as linguistics, computer science, artificial intelligence, and machine learning that helps computers to understand, interpret, generate, and interact with human language in a way that humans do. NLP helps in transforming unstructured language data into meaningful insights and actions. This chapter will provide insights into fundamental concepts that underlie NLP, helping computers to navigate the details of language and derive meaningful information from it.

The applications of NLP are vast, spanning industries from business to the health domain, including creating virtual assistants, creating business solutions, among others. In this chapter, we will discuss real-world applications of NLP, unveiling its role in revolutionizing customer service, healthcare diagnostics, content recommendation, and more. By understanding these applications, we gain insight into the tangible impact NLP has on our daily experiences.

Although the field of NLP has achieved success, it still comprises many challenges. These include ambiguities, idioms, and context. This chapter will discuss the multifaceted challenges of NLP, such as disambiguation, domain adaptation, and ethical considerations.

This introductory chapter helps us to explore the intricate interplay between language and technology. In the subsequent chapters, we will unveil the mechanisms, methodologies, and tools that enable us to harness the power of NLP and help us develop in the new era of human-computer interaction.

Structure

In this chapter, we will discuss the following topics:

- Understanding NLP
- Applications of NLP
- NLP Challenges and Approaches

Understanding NLP

Natural Language Processing (NLP) is one of the fields under linguistics, computer science, and artificial intelligence that helps to bridge the large gap between human language and machine understanding. NLP helps in empowering computers to comprehend, interpret, generate, and communicate in human languages, such as English, Spanish, Chinese, and beyond. NLP equips machines with the ability to process, analyze, and respond to written texts as well as spoken information, thereby enabling them to interact with humans in a manner that is both intuitive and contextually relevant.

Linguistic Foundations

Human languages are morphologically rich and complex, comprising homonyms, idioms, cultural references, and contextual variations that provide different meanings. NLP researchers draw inspiration from linguistics to understand sentence structures, syntax, semantics, and pragmatics. This linguistic foundation allows machines to decipher the intended meaning of a sentence beyond its literal interpretation.

Computational Challenges

Despite multiple applications of NLP, there are vast complexities associated with the language. Language evolves over time, varies across regions, and changes based on the context and intent of communication. As such, NLP faces a series of challenges that make the task of processing and understanding language far from straightforward. These are mentioned as follows:

- **Ambiguity**: Many words and phrases possess multiple meanings, and their correct interpretation depends on the context in which they are used.
- **Syntax and Grammar**: Languages follow certain rules of syntax and grammar that decide how words are structured and combined to form meaningful sentences. Following these rules in a computational framework requires an understanding of linguistic structures.
- **Semantics**: Understanding the meaning of words and sentences is vital. This involves recognizing synonyms, antonyms, analogies, and the implications of different word choices.
- **Context**: Context plays an important role in language comprehension. Words can take on different meanings depending on the context of the conversation. For example, the word *orange* could refer to a fruit or the name of a color.
- **Cultural and Domain Specificity**: Language is influenced by cultural, regional, and domain-specific aspects. Slang, idioms, and domain-specific jargon can present challenges for machines unfamiliar with these variations.
- **Sentiment and Tone**: Recognizing sentiment, emotions, and tones in text is essential for understanding the underlying emotions and attitudes in communication.

NLP Techniques and Approaches

NLP involves the following techniques and approaches, often drawing from machine learning and artificial intelligence, to overcome these challenges:

- **Tokenization**: Breaking text into smaller units, such as words or subwords, is the first step. This process, known as tokenization, forms the basis for subsequent analysis.
- **Part-of-Speech Tagging**: Assigning part-of-speech categories to words in a sentence, such as nouns, verbs, adjectives, and adverbs, helps establish sentence structure.
- **Named Entity Recognition (NER)**: Identifying named entities such as names of people, places, organizations, and dates is important for understanding context and has numerous applications such as Machine Translation, Text Summarization, Question Answering Systems, and so on.
- **Word Embeddings**: Representing words as dense numerical vectors captures semantic relationships, enabling machines to understand word similarities and context.
- **Machine Learning Models**: We can apply various Machine Learning Models such as Supervised Learning, Unsupervised Learning, or Reinforcement Learning on an unstructured text to perform various NLP tasks on it.

- **Neural Networks**: Deep learning, particularly with the use of neural networks, has revolutionized NLP. **Recurrent Neural Networks (RNNs), Convolutional Neural Networks (CNNs)**, and Transformer-based models such as BERT and GPT have significantly improved language understanding.

NLP is a dynamic and rapidly evolving field that is a result of modern interaction and technology. Its ability to imbue machines with language comprehension and generation capabilities has enabled groundbreaking applications across diverse domains. From chatbots that simulate human conversation to language translation that connects global communities, NLP continues to reshape the boundaries of what machines can achieve in understanding and working with human language.

NLP's impact is vast and diverse, shaping various sectors, as follows:

- **Communication and Interaction**: Chatbots, virtual assistants, and sentiment analysis tools enable seamless human-machine conversations.
- **Information Retrieval**: Search engines use NLP to understand user queries and deliver relevant results.
- **Translation**: NLP powers real-time language translation, bridging linguistic divides.
- **Healthcare and Diagnostics**: NLP assists in medical record analysis and diagnoses through textual data.
- **Finance and Market Analysis**: Sentiment analysis aids in predicting market trends.

Applications of NLP

The applications of NLP span a diverse range of industries and domains, transforming the way we interact with technology and enabling machines to comprehend, interpret, and generate human language. From communication and automation to insights and decision-making, NLP has provided a new era of innovation. Here is a detailed discussion of its various applications:

- **Chatbots and Virtual Assistants**: NLP provides interactive chatbots and virtual assistants that are involved in natural conversations with users. These systems are involved in customer service, provide instant responses to queries, troubleshoot issues, and make user experiences on websites and messaging platforms better with time.
- **Language Translation**: NLP-driven machine translation has broken down language barriers, facilitating seamless communication between individuals and cultures. Applications such as Google Translate use NLP techniques to translate text and speech from one language to another, enabling global collaboration.

- **Information Retrieval and Search Engines**: Search engines use NLP to understand user queries and retrieve relevant information from vast amounts of online content. The accuracy of search results is greatly improved through techniques such as semantic analysis and contextual understanding.
- **Sentiment Analysis**: NLP tools analyze text to gauge the sentiment or emotional tone expressed within it. This is extensively used in social media monitoring, market research, and customer feedback analysis to understand public opinions, attitudes, and trends.
- **Text Summarization**: NLP helps in the generation of concise and coherent summaries of lengthy texts. This is valuable in areas including news articles, research papers, and legal documents, where quickly extracting key information is essential.
- **Named Entity Recognition (NER)**: NER identifies and categorizes entities such as names of people, organizations, dates, and locations within a text. This has applications in information extraction, document categorization, and more.
- **Speech Recognition**: NLP-powered speech recognition technology converts spoken language into written text. It is used in voice assistants, transcription services, voice search, and accessibility tools for individuals with disabilities.
- **Question Answering Systems**: These systems use NLP to understand user questions and provide accurate answers from vast amounts of text data. They are used in information retrieval, virtual assistants, and educational platforms.
- **Automatic Language Generation**: NLP models can generate human-like text, which finds applications in content creation, creative writing, and even generating code.
- **Healthcare and Clinical Text Analysis**: NLP assists in analyzing medical records, clinical notes, and research papers, extracting insights for medical diagnoses, treatment recommendations, and research findings.
- **Financial and Market Analysis**: Sentiment analysis and text mining are employed in analyzing financial news, social media, and reports to predict market trends, investor sentiment, and business insights.
- **Legal and Compliance Analysis**: NLP aids in reviewing legal documents, contracts, and regulatory compliance documents, helping legal professionals quickly identify relevant information and insights.
- **Content Recommendations**: NLP-related recommendation systems analyze user preferences and behaviors to suggest personalized content, products, and services, enhancing user engagement and satisfaction.
- **Language Tutoring and Learning**: NLP can provide language learners with interactive exercises, grammar correction, and personalized feedback, aiding in language acquisition.

- **Crisis Management and Emergency Response**: NLP assists in analyzing social media and news feeds and helps in monitoring real-time events, helping authorities to respond effectively to crises and emergencies.
- **Content Curation and Personalization**: NLP is used to construct content for users based on their preferences, behaviors, and historical interactions. This personalization enhances user engagement on platforms such as social media, news websites, and streaming services.
- **Emotion Recognition and Mental Health Support**: NLP aids in detecting emotional states from text, enabling applications that offer emotional support, detect signs of distress, and provide resources for mental health assistance.
- **Social Media Analysis and Trend Prediction**: NLP analyzes social media posts, comments, and interactions to identify emerging trends, monitor brand sentiment, and assess public response to events.
- **Resume Screening and Job Matching**: NLP assists in scanning resumes and job descriptions to match candidates with job openings, aiding in the recruitment process.
- **Fake News Detection**: NLP algorithms can recognize misleading or false information in news articles and social media posts, helping to fight against misinformation.
- **Language Translation for Literature and Research**: NLP-driven translation facilitates the dissemination of literature, research papers, and academic resources across languages, fostering global collaboration.
- **Automatic Email Responses and Sorting**: NLP helps in the automatic categorization of emails, sorting them into folders, and generating contextually appropriate responses, enhancing email management.
- **Medical Data Mining and Literature Review**: NLP helps in extracting relevant information from medical literature, helping researchers stay up-to-date with advancements in their field.
- **Legal Document Analysis and e-Discovery**: NLP helps in speeding up the review of legal documents during e-discovery to identify important information related to litigation and compliance tasks.
- **Government and Public Services**: NLP enhances public services by analyzing citizen feedback, automating responses, and aiding in sentiment analysis of public opinion.
- **Pharmaceutical Research and Drug Development**: NLP supports researchers in analyzing vast volumes of scientific literature, aiding in drug discovery, development, and safety monitoring.
- **Language Accessibility for Disabilities**: NLP assists individuals with visual or hearing impairments by converting text to speech or generating captions,

enhancing accessibility.

- **Human Resources and Employee Feedback**: NLP analyzes employee feedback, surveys, and sentiment to provide insights into organizational culture, engagement, and well-being.
- **Academic Plagiarism Detection**: NLP algorithms compare texts to a database of existing literature to detect instances of plagiarism in academic and professional writing.

The applications of NLP continue to increase across industries, domains, and aspects of our daily lives. As NLP technologies evolve, their potential to enhance communication, automate tasks, and provide valuable insights becomes even more profound. This dynamic field promises a future where machines and humans communicate seamlessly, unlocking new realms of productivity, creativity, and understanding.

NLP Challenges and Approaches

NLP is a complex field that involves huge challenges. Researchers and practitioners in NLP employ a variety of approaches and techniques to address these challenges, enabling machines to better understand, process, and generate human language. Let us delve into some of the prominent challenges in NLP and the corresponding approaches used to overcome them:

- **Lexical Ambiguity:** Lexical Ambiguity involves that many words have multiple meanings, and determining the correct sense based on context is a significant challenge in NLP.

  Contextual analysis, utilizing adjacent words and broader sentence context, is employed to disambiguate word meanings. Word embeddings capture semantic relationships between words and can assist in distinguishing various senses.

- **Contextual Understanding:** Words can have different meanings based on the surrounding context, requiring a deeper understanding of the discourse.

  Approaches used for contextual understanding are machine learning models, particularly contextual models such as transformers, capture contextual information across sentences, paragraphs, and documents, aiding in accurate understanding.

- **Named Entity Recognition (NER):** Named Entity Recognition means identifying and categorizing entities such as names, dates, and locations within text for context comprehension.

  Approaches used for NER are pattern recognition or gazetteer approach, machine learning, and rule-based techniques to identify and classify entities within text.

- **Coreference Resolution:** Coreference Resolution means recognizing when different words or phrases refer to the same entity within a text.

  Approaches used for coreference resolution involve linguistic analysis to determine entity references and employ machine learning models that consider surrounding words and context.
- **Sentiment Analysis:** Sentiment Analysis involves detecting nuanced sentiments, sarcasm, and emotional tone in the text. Sentiment analysis employs machine learning models trained on labeled data to identify sentiment-bearing words and phrases, capturing both explicit and implied emotions.
- **Language Variation:** Languages vary across dialects, regions, and cultures, making it difficult to build models that generalize effectively. Data augmentation, transfer learning, and multi-dialectal training are used to adapt models to different linguistic variations.
- **Data Scarcity and Low Resource Languages:** Some languages lack sufficient data for robust NLP model training, hindering their application in these languages. Few-shot and zero-shot learning techniques, along with cross-lingual transfer learning, enable models to perform tasks with limited training data.
- **Ethical and Bias Challenges**
  - **Challenge**: NLP models can inadvertently perpetuate biases present in training data, leading to fairness and ethical concerns.
  - **Approaches**: Researchers are developing methods to identify and mitigate bias in NLP models, emphasizing fairness, transparency, and bias-aware training.
- **Multilingual Understanding**
  - **Challenge**: Models that perform well in one language may not generalize effectively to other languages.
  - **Approaches**: Multilingual models leverage shared linguistic properties across languages, enabling the transfer of knowledge from one language to another.
- **Explainability and Interpretability**
  - **Challenge**: Understanding why NLP models make certain predictions or decisions can be challenging, especially in complex models such as transformers.
  - **Approaches**: Efforts are directed toward developing techniques that provide insight into model decision-making, offering explanations for model outputs.

- **Multimodal Challenges**

  Integrating multiple forms of data, such as text and images, poses challenges in creating models that can effectively process and interpret these diverse modalities.

  Multimodal models include information from different modalities, utilizing techniques such as image captioning and text-to-image synthesis.

NLP challenges are manifold, and the field is constantly evolving to address them. Approaches often involve a combination of linguistic insights, machine-learning techniques, and domain-specific knowledge. As NLP continues to progress, the community's efforts in tackling these challenges pave the way for more accurate, robust, and ethical language technologies.

Conclusion

NLP bridges the gap between human language and computational power. This chapter has taken us on a journey through the captivating landscape of NLP, unveiling its significance, challenges, and transformative applications.

From the various layers of linguistic understanding to the complexities of word ambiguity, context comprehension, and sentiment analysis, we have explored the myriad challenges that NLP confronts. Each challenge serves as a testament to the richness and nuances of human language, a testament that NLP researchers and practitioners embrace as they strive to enable machines to master the subtleties of language.

In our exploration of NLP's techniques and approaches, we have witnessed the fusion of linguistics and cutting-edge technology. Tokenization, word embeddings, neural networks, and pre-trained models have all played a pivotal role in pushing the boundaries of NLP's capabilities. With these tools in hand, we have ventured into a realm where machines understand sentiments, generate human-like text, and converse with users in ways that were once confined to human-human interactions.

The extensive applications of NLP traverse industries and domains, transforming the way we communicate, learn, do business, and access information. From chatbots facilitating customer support to language translation breaking language barriers, NLP's impact is woven into the fabric of modern life. The future holds even more possibilities, where NLP might aid in human well-being, ethical decision-making, and deeper cross-cultural understanding.

NLP is not just a field; it is a bridge between humans and machines, uniting our capacity for language with the computational prowess of artificial intelligence. It is a field that raises questions about understanding, creativity, ethics, and the very essence of communication. NLP beckons us to continue exploring its depths, conquering challenges, and unlocking the potential of language for the betterment of society and technology alike.

In the next chapter, we will discuss PyTorch, its installation, and GPU acceleration with PyTorch.

Points to Remember

- Natural Language Processing (NLP) is a process of making machines generate, understand, and analyze human language.
- NLP involves a combination of fields such as AI, linguistics, and computational methods that can bridge the gap between humans and technology.
- NLP involves the collection of tasks such as phonology, syntactic analysis, semantic analysis, and pragmatics.
- NLP involves contextual understanding as well as understanding emotional expressions.
- Lexical ambiguity refers to a word having multiple meanings.
- Tokenization is the process of breaking text into meaningful units.
- Named Entity Recognition (NER) involves the recognition of entities such as names, organizations, locations, and so on.
- NLP faces challenges such as lexical ambiguity, contextual understanding, bias, and coreference resolution.
- NLP is a branch of science that bridges the gap as to how humans interact with machines.

Multiple Choice Questions

1. What is the primary goal of Natural Language Processing (NLP)?
   a. Enhancing human-animal communication
   b. Enabling machines to understand and process human language
   c. Developing faster computer hardware
   d. Improving weather prediction
2. Which aspect of language does NLP focus on when dealing with word meanings and relationships?
   a. Phonology
   b. Syntax

   c. Semantics

   d. Pragmatics

3. What challenge in NLP involves recognizing when different words refer to the same entity?

   a. Sentiment analysis

   b. Coreference resolution

   c. Named Entity Recognition (NER)

   d. Lexical ambiguity

4. How do NLP models address the challenge of word sense ambiguity?

   a. By ignoring the context

   b. By using rule-based techniques only

   c. By analyzing surrounding words and context

   d. By selecting the first possible meaning

5. Which technique is used to represent words in high-dimensional vectors, capturing semantic relationships?

   a. Contextual analysis

   b. Tokenization

   c. Word embeddings

   d. Coreference resolution

6. Which application of NLP involves the translation of text from one language to another?

   a. Sentiment analysis

   b. Content recommendation

   c. Language translation

   d. Named Entity Recognition (NER)

7. What is the challenge in NLP related to understanding implied emotions and tones?

   a. Contextual understanding

   b. Word sense disambiguation

    c. Sentiment analysis
    d. Ethical considerations

8. Which advancement in NLP enables models to leverage knowledge from one task to improve performance in another?
    a. Transfer learning
    b. Machine translation
    c. Sentiment analysis
    d. Lexical ambiguity

9. What is the primary focus of explainability and interpretability in NLP?
    a. Detecting named entities
    b. Understanding context
    c. Providing insights into model decisions
    d. Identifying sarcasm and irony

10. What does NLP's future hold?
    a. NLP will be replaced by traditional linguistic methods
    b. NLP will focus solely on syntax analysis
    c. NLP will become obsolete due to language barriers
    d. NLP will advance with deeper language understanding and ethical considerations

Answers

1. b
2. c
3. b
4. c
5. c
6. c
7. c

8. a
9. c
10. d

Questions

1. What is the role of Natural Language Processing (NLP) in bridging the gap that lies between human language and emerging technology?
2. What are the challenges faced in lexical ambiguity in NLP? How can these challenges be overcome?
3. Explain with examples the importance of contextual understanding in enhancing textual comprehension by machines.
4. What are the applications of NLP in the healthcare domain? How can medical data analysis using NLP provide improvement in a patient's health?
5. Explain transformer-based models, such as BERT and GPT, used in NLP. Explain the concept of transfer learning and its importance in NLP.
6. How is NLP used in sentiment analysis? Explain its applications.
7. Explain the concept of coreference resolution in NLP. How do NLP models identify and resolve instances where different words refer to the same entity?
8. What are the applications of NLP in education today? How can NLP be used in enhancing language learning experiences for students?
9. Explain the applications and advancements in AI-based conversational systems.

Key Terms

- **Natural Language Processing (NLP)**: The branch of science that deals with the interpretation, understanding, and generation of natural language by machines.
- **Lexical Ambiguity**: It refers to the existence of words with different meanings, and it requires their interpretation based on the given context.
- **Sentiment Analysis**: It refers to the identification of sentiment or emotion from a given text on the basis of attitude, mood, or opinions.
- **Coreference Resolution**: It refers to the process when different expressions or words refer to the same entity in a text.

- **Named Entity Recognition (NER)**: The process of recognizing named entities in a given text and categorizing them into different named entity classes, such as name, location, organization, dates, and so on.
- **Sentiment Detection**: It is one of the subtasks of sentiment analysis that involves the recognition of sentiments, such as positive, negative, or neutral, from a given text expression.
- **Tokenization**: It refers to the process of dividing a given text into individual units or tokens.
- **Content Generation**: It is the process of the creation of text with the help of NLP techniques.

Chapter 2
Getting Started with PyTorch

Introduction

In this chapter, we embark on a journey into the era of PyTorch, a versatile and commonly used open-source machine learning framework. PyTorch 2.2 is the latest version of this framework that is built on the predecessor's success, and it has several enhancements, making it an excellent choice for the development of applications based on natural language processing (NLP).

As we delve into this chapter, we will explore the fundamental aspects of PyTorch 2.2, from its installation to its core concepts and capabilities. This chapter provides us with the essential knowledge and tools we need to harness the power of PyTorch for NLP.

This chapter begins by introducing PyTorch 2.2, highlighting its significance. It will guide you through the installation process, ensuring that you have a fully functional PyTorch environment set up, in which we will delve into the basics of PyTorch, including tensors and operations, which form the foundation of all PyTorch-based NLP projects.

In the final section of this chapter, we will show you how to harness the computational prowess of GPUs to supercharge your NLP applications.

By the end of this chapter, you will have a solid grasp of PyTorch's fundamentals and be well-prepared to dive into the exciting world of natural language processing with PyTorch 2.2.

Structure

In this chapter, we will discuss the following topics:

- Introduction to PyTorch
- Installing PyTorch 2.0

- PyTorch Basics
  - Tensors and Operations
- GPU Acceleration with PyTorch

Introduction to PyTorch

In this section, we will explore PyTorch, a dynamic and versatile deep learning framework that has gained popularity in the machine learning community. PyTorch stands out for its flexibility, ease of use, and dynamic computation graph, making it an excellent choice for both beginners and experienced practitioners in the field of artificial intelligence and natural language processing.

The Significance of PyTorch

PyTorch has become important in the world of deep learning as well, and its significance cannot be overstated. Developed by Facebook's AI Research lab (FAIR), PyTorch has played a pivotal role in advancing the field of deep learning and NLP. Its dynamic computation graph, which allows for intuitive model building and debugging, has won the hearts of researchers and developers worldwide.

The release of PyTorch 2.2 has further elevated the framework's capabilities, introducing new features, optimizations, and improvements. It continues to empower individuals and organizations to push the boundaries of what is possible in NLP and other AI domains.

Key Highlights

As we venture deeper into this chapter, we will uncover several key aspects of PyTorch:

- **Flexibility**: PyTorch's dynamic computation graph enables dynamic changes to the models. This flexibility is valuable when we are applying it, especially to NLP architectures.
- **Community and Resources**: PyTorch boasts a vibrant and welcoming community. Abundant resources, tutorials, and third-party libraries are easily available, making it easier for everyone to learn and apply PyTorch effectively.
- **Deep Learning for NLP**: PyTorch has become the framework of choice for many state-of-the-art NLP models. Its flexible nature has led to the development of models such as Transformers, which have revolutionized NLP tasks.
- **Ecosystem**: PyTorch has an ecosystem of tools and libraries, such as PyTorch Lightning, Transformers, and TorchText, that are designed to streamline NLP tasks.

In the following sections of this chapter, we will go through the installation process of PyTorch. We will explore the fundamental concepts that underpin PyTorch, including tensors and operations. Finally, we will delve into harnessing the power of GPUs for accelerated deep learning computations.

Installing PyTorch 2.0

Setting up PyTorch 2.2 is an important step in our journey towards applying natural language processing techniques with the latest tools and libraries. In this section, we will provide a comprehensive guide on how to install PyTorch 2.2 based on your specific needs and environment.

Prerequisites

Before we begin the installation process, it is essential to ensure you have the necessary prerequisites in place:

- **Python**: PyTorch is primarily a Python library. Therefore, you should have Python installed on your system. We recommend using Python 3.6 or later to ensure compatibility with the latest PyTorch version.
- **Package Manager**: You will need a package manager to install PyTorch. The two most common package managers for Python are **`pip`** and **`conda`**. Make sure you have one of them installed on your system.

Installing PyTorch via `pip`

For many users, pip is the preferred method for installing Python packages, including PyTorch. Here are the steps to install PyTorch 2.2 via **`pip`**:

CPU Version Installation

To install the CPU version of PyTorch, open your terminal or command prompt and run the following command:

```
pip install torch==2.2.0
```

This command will download and install the latest stable release of PyTorch 2.2 for CPU computation.

Installing PyTorch

After the installation of Python, it is essential to verify that PyTorch is correctly installed. Open a Python interpreter or create a Python script and run the following commands to ensure that PyTorch is accessible:

```
import torch
print(torch.__version__)  # This should print '2.2.0'
```

This code imports PyTorch and prints its version. If you see '2.2.0' displayed, your installation was successful.

If you encounter any issues during the installation process, such as compatibility problems or dependency conflicts, refer to the official PyTorch documentation (https://pytorch.org/get-started/locally/) for troubleshooting tips and additional installation options.

With PyTorch successfully installed, you are now equipped with the essential tools to explore its fundamentals and embark on your journey into the world of natural language processing using PyTorch 2.2. In the following sections of this chapter, we will delve deeper into PyTorch's core concepts and demonstrate how to leverage its power for NLP tasks.

PyTorch Basics

In this section, we will discuss the basics of PyTorch in detail. Let us begin.

Tensors and Operations

Now that we have PyTorch 2.2 installed, it is time to dive into the fundamentals of this powerful deep learning framework. PyTorch is renowned for its simplicity and flexibility, making it an ideal choice for researchers and developers working on NLP projects. In this section, we will cover the core concepts you need to understand before delving into more advanced topics.

Tensors: The Building Blocks

At the heart of PyTorch are tensors. Tensors are multi-dimensional arrays that can hold data of various types, including integers, floating-point numbers, and even more complex data structures. You can think of tensors as the building blocks of neural networks and the foundation of PyTorch's numerical computations.

Creating Tensors

Let us start by creating a few tensors. In PyTorch, you can create tensors using the **`torch.Tensor`** constructor or by converting existing Python lists or NumPy arrays into tensors:

```
import torch
# Create a tensor from a list
tensor_a = torch.tensor([1, 2, 3])
# Create a tensor filled with zeros
tensor_zeros = torch.zeros(2, 3)
# Create a tensor filled with ones
tensor_ones = torch.ones(2, 3)
# Create a tensor with random values
tensor_random = torch.rand(2, 3)
print(tensor_a)
tensor([1, 2, 3])
print(tensor_zeros)
tensor([[0., 0., 0.],
        [0., 0., 0.]])
print(tensor_ones)
tensor([[1., 1., 1.],
        [1., 1., 1.]])
print(tensor_random)
tensor([[0.3856, 0.3199, 0.3250],
        [0.2133, 0.7103, 0.1877]])
```

Tensor Operations

Once you have tensors, you can perform various operations on them, such as addition, subtraction, multiplication, and more. PyTorch provides a rich set of functions for these operations:

```
# Element-wise addition
result = tensor_a + tensor_a
print(result)
tensor([2, 4, 6])

# Element-wise multiplication
result = tensor_a * 2
print(result)
tensor([2, 4, 6])

# Matrix multiplication
matrix_a = torch.tensor([[1, 2], [3, 4]])
print(matrix_a)
tensor([[1, 2],
        [3, 4]])
matrix_b = torch.tensor([[5, 6], [7, 8]])
print(matrix_b)
tensor([[5, 6],
        [7, 8]])
```

```
result = torch.matmul(matrix_a, matrix_b)
print(result)
tensor([[19, 22],
        [43, 50]])
```

Autograd: Automatic Differentiation

One of PyTorch's standout features is its automatic differentiation library, known as Autograd. Autograd enables PyTorch to automatically compute gradients for tensors, making it incredibly useful for training neural networks through techniques such as gradient descent.

```
import torch
# Define a tensor with requires_grad=True to track gradients
x = torch.tensor(2.0, requires_grad=True)
print(x)
tensor(2., requires_grad=True)

# Perform operations on the tensor
y = x**2 + 3*x + 1
print(y)
tensor(11., grad_fn=<AddBackward0>)
# Compute gradients
y.backward()
# Access the gradients
gradient = x.grad
print(gradient)
tensor(7.)
```

The **`requires_grad`** attribute tells PyTorch to track operations on the tensor and compute gradients. The **`backward()`** method computes gradients, and you can access them using the **`.grad`** attribute.

Neural Networks with PyTorch

Neural networks in PyTorch are typically built using the **`torch.nn`** module. This module provides classes and functions to create and train neural network architectures, including layers such as linear layers, convolutional layers, and recurrent layers.

A Feedforward Neural Network (FNN) is a type of artificial neural network. In FNN, there is an input layer, an output layer, and many hidden layers. There is no cycle in FNN. This network is referred to as feedforward since information flows only in a forward direction, from input to output.

```
import torch
import torch.nn as nn
# Define a simple feedforward neural network
```

```
class SimpleNet(nn.Module):
    def __init__(self):
        super(SimpleNet, self).__init__()
        self.fc1 = nn.Linear(64, 128)
        self.fc2 = nn.Linear(128, 10)

    def forward(self, x):
        x = torch.relu(self.fc1(x))
        x = self.fc2(x)
        return x
# Create an instance of the network
net = SimpleNet()
```

Here, we define a simple feedforward neural network using PyTorch's neural network module. We specify the layers in the **`__init__`** method and define the forward pass in the forward method.

Training a Neural Network

To train a neural network in PyTorch, you typically follow these steps:

1. Define a loss function to measure the model's performance.
2. Choose an optimization algorithm (for example, Stochastic Gradient Descent) to update the model's parameters.
3. Iterate through your dataset, computing predictions, loss, and gradients, and then update the model's weights.

PyTorch provides a convenient interface for performing these steps. In the following example, we have used the NumPy library to load the dataset and the PyTorch library for using deep learning models. We have converted NumPy arrays into tensors. In this example, the sigmoid function is used in the output, which ensures the output value is between 0 and 1. Training a neural network means setting the model weights that map the input with the required output. Optimizer is an algorithm used to adjust the weights in a neural network model. In this example, we have used the Adam algorithm as an optimizer. The term epoch means when a complete dataset is sent to a model for training. The term batch means a few samples of the dataset are sent to the model for training as a part of the iteration. Here is a simplified example:

```
import numpy as np
import torch
import torch.nn as nn
import torch.optim as optim

# load the dataset, split into input (X) and output (y) variables
dataset = np.loadtxt('/Users/pramuditkhurana/Downloads/a.csv',
delimiter=',')
```

```
X = dataset[:,0:8]
y = dataset[:,8]

X = torch.tensor(X, dtype=torch.float32)
y = torch.tensor(y, dtype=torch.float32).reshape(-1, 1)

# define the model
model = nn.Sequential(
    nn.Linear(8, 12),
    nn.ReLU(),
    nn.Linear(12, 8),
    nn.ReLU(),
    nn.Linear(8, 1),
    nn.Sigmoid()
)
print(model)

# train the model
lossfun   = nn.BCELoss()  # binary cross entropy
optimizer = optim.Adam(model.parameters(), lr=0.001)

n_epochs = 100
batch_size = 10

for epoch in range(n_epochs):
    for i in range(0, len(X), batch_size):
        Xbatch = X[i:i+batch_size]
        y_pred = model(Xbatch)
        ybatch = y[i:i+batch_size]
        loss = lossfun(y_pred, ybatch)
        optimizer.zero_grad()
        loss.backward()
        optimizer.step()
    print(f'Finished epoch {epoch}, latest loss {loss}')

# compute accuracy (no_grad is optional)
with torch.no_grad():
    y_pred = model(X)
accuracy = (y_pred.round() == y).float().mean()
print(f"Accuracy {accuracy}")
```

The output for the preceding code is as follows:

```
Sequential(
  (0): Linear(in_features=8, out_features=12, bias=True)
  (1): ReLU()
  (2): Linear(in_features=12, out_features=8, bias=True)
  (3): ReLU()
```

```
  (4): Linear(in_features=8, out_features=1, bias=True)
  (5): Sigmoid()
)
Finished epoch 0, latest loss 0.5982971787452698
Finished epoch 1, latest loss 0.5270138382911682
Finished epoch 2, latest loss 0.49896082282066345
…….

Finished epoch 98, latest loss 0.5651640892028809
Finished epoch 99, latest loss 0.556884229183197
Accuracy 0.7747395634651184

                                                                  In [ ]:
```

In this example, we use a simple feedforward neural network (SimpleNet), a cross-entropy loss function, and Stochastic Gradient Descent (SGD) as the optimizer. We iterate through the dataset, compute predictions, calculate the loss, perform backpropagation to compute gradients, and update the model's weights using the optimizer.

These are the foundational concepts of PyTorch that you will build upon as you progress in your NLP journey. In the following sections of this chapter, we will explore more advanced topics and demonstrate how to apply these concepts to natural language processing tasks using PyTorch 2.2.

GPU Acceleration with PyTorch

One of the key advantages of using PyTorch for deep learning is its seamless integration with Graphics Processing Units (GPUs). GPUs are highly specialized hardware designed for parallel processing, making them ideal for accelerating the computationally intensive operations involved in training deep neural networks. In this section, we will delve into how you can harness the power of GPUs to supercharge your natural language processing (NLP) tasks in PyTorch.

The Need to Use GPUs

GPUs offer significant advantages over Central Processing Units (CPUs) when it comes to deep learning tasks:

- **Parallelism**: GPUs consist of thousands of small cores that can perform multiple calculations simultaneously. This parallelism accelerates matrix operations, which are fundamental to deep learning.
- **Speed**: GPUs are optimized for numerical computations, providing a substantial speedup for training neural networks. Tasks that might take days on a CPU can be completed in hours or even minutes on a GPU.

- **Memory**: Modern GPUs come equipped with large amounts of high-speed memory, allowing you to work with larger datasets and more complex models.

Checking for GPU Availability

Before you can take advantage of GPU acceleration in PyTorch, you need to ensure that your system has a compatible NVIDIA GPU and that you have installed the GPU version of PyTorch during the installation process.

You can check if PyTorch is currently configured to use a GPU by running the following code:

```
import torch
# Check if CUDA (GPU support) is available
cuda_available = torch.cuda.is_available()
# Get the name of the GPU (if available)if cuda_available:
    gpu_name = torch.cuda.get_device_name(0)  # Assuming one GPU is
available
```

This code checks if CUDA (NVIDIA's parallel computing platform and API) is available and, if so, retrieves the name of the GPU.

Moving Tensors to GPU

In PyTorch, you can easily move tensors between CPU and GPU using the **`.to()`** method. Here is how you can move a tensor to the GPU:

```
import torch
# Create a tensor on the CPU
cpu_tensor = torch.tensor([1, 2, 3])
# Move the tensor to the GPU (if available)
if torch.cuda.is_available():
    gpu_tensor = cpu_tensor.to('cuda')
```

Keep in mind that the GPU tensor retains its original data type (for example, float32), so you may need to convert it to the appropriate data type before performing operations if your CPU and GPU tensors have different data types.

GPU Accelerated Training

Once your data and model are on the GPU, PyTorch automatically performs computations on the GPU, making the training process significantly faster. For example, consider the following code snippet:

```
import torch
import torch.nn as nn
import torch.optim as optim
```

```
# Create a neural network and move it to the GPU
model = MyNLPModel()
model.to('cuda')
# Define loss function and optimizer
criterion = nn.CrossEntropyLoss()
optimizer = optim.Adam(model.parameters(), lr=0.001)
# Training loop for epoch in range(epochs):
    for inputs, labels in dataloader:
        # Move data to GPU
        inputs, labels = inputs.to('cuda'), labels.to('cuda')
        optimizer.zero_grad()
        outputs = model(inputs)
        loss = criterion(outputs, labels)
        loss.backward()
        optimizer.step()
```

In this example, the neural network (model), input data (inputs), and labels (labels) are all moved to the GPU. The training loop then performs all computations on the GPU, resulting in faster training times.

GPU Considerations

While GPU acceleration can dramatically speed up deep learning tasks, there are a few considerations to keep in mind:

- **GPU Memory**: GPUs have limited memory, so larger models and datasets may exceed available memory. You may need to batch your data or use techniques such as gradient accumulation to work with such cases.
- **GPU Availability**: Not all users or cloud platforms have access to powerful GPUs. Be aware of resource constraints when developing and deploying your NLP models.
- **Data Transfer Overhead:** Moving data between CPU and GPU incurs a slight overhead. Minimize unnecessary data transfers to optimize performance.
- **Mixed Precision Training**: Modern GPUs support mixed precision training, which uses lower-precision data types for faster training without sacrificing accuracy.

In conclusion, GPU acceleration with PyTorch plays a significant role in NLP, allowing you to train and deploy models faster and tackle more complex tasks. By understanding how to utilize GPUs effectively in your PyTorch workflow, you can harness the full potential of deep learning for natural language processing.

Conclusion

In this chapter, we began by understanding the significance of PyTorch in the field of deep learning and NLP. PyTorch's flexibility, dynamic computation graph, and strong community support make it a compelling choice for NLP practitioners. We covered the installation of PyTorch 2.2, ensuring that you have a functional environment to work with. Whether you installed the CPU or GPU version, you are now equipped with the tools to dive deeper into PyTorch. We explored the fundamental concepts of PyTorch, focusing on tensors as the building blocks of numerical computations. We learned how to create tensors, perform operations on them, and leverage PyTorch's automatic differentiation capabilities through Autograd. We also introduced the basics of building neural networks using PyTorch's nn module and demonstrated how to train a simple neural network.

Lastly, we uncovered the power of GPU acceleration for deep learning tasks in PyTorch. We discussed the advantages of using GPUs, checked for GPU availability, and learned how to move data and models between the CPU and GPU. GPU acceleration is a game changer for NLP, enabling faster training and more complex models. In the next chapter, we will discuss Text Preprocessing tasks such as tokenization, stop word removal, stemming and lemmatization, handling special characters and punctuation, and word embeddings and Word2Vec.

Points to Remember

- PyTorch is an open-source machine learning framework developed by Facebook's AI Research lab (FAIR).
- PyTorch features dynamic computation graphs, making it flexible for various applications.
- Installation typically involves using package managers such as pip or conda.
- Ensure you have the correct Python version (commonly Python 3.x) installed.
- PyTorch provides a NumPy-like interface for working with data.
- Tensors can be created from lists, NumPy arrays, or generated with random values.
- PyTorch supports element-wise tensor operations similar to NumPy.
- Using GPUs significantly speeds up computation in deep learning tasks.

Multiple Choice Questions

1. What is PyTorch primarily used for?
    a. Image processing
    b. Web development
    c. Deep learning and neural networks
    d. Game development

2. How do you typically install PyTorch?
   a. Using the "`pip`" package manager
   b. Using the "`npm`" package manager
   c. Downloading a standalone installer
   d. Manually compiling the source code
3. Which of the following is NOT a core component of PyTorch?
   a. Tensors
   b. Dynamic computation graphs
   c. DataFrames
   d. Neural networks
4. In PyTorch, what data structure is similar to NumPy arrays and serves as the fundamental building block for computations?
   a. Lists
   b. Arrays
   c. Tensors
   d. DataFrames
5. What is the key benefit of using PyTorch's dynamic computation graphs?
   a. Faster execution of code
   b. Simplicity and ease of use
   c. Flexibility for various applications
   d. Compatibility with TensorFlow
6. How can you move a PyTorch tensor to a GPU for acceleration?
   a. By running a separate GPU-related installation command
   b. Using the `.to()` or `.cuda()` method
   c. Manually rewriting the code to target the GPU
   d. PyTorch does not support GPU acceleration
7. Which Python version is commonly used when working with PyTorch?
   a. Python 2.x
   b. Python 3.x
   c. Python 4.x
   d. Python 5.x

8. What type of operations are typically performed on PyTorch tensors?
    a. Matrix multiplications
    b. Element-wise operations
    c. String manipulations
    d. Graph algorithms

Answers

1. c
2. a
3. c
4. c
5. c
6. b
7. b
8. b

Questions

1. Describe the key differences between PyTorch and static computation graph-based frameworks such as TensorFlow. How do these differences impact the flexibility of PyTorch?
2. Can you walk through the installation process of PyTorch 2.0 on a specific operating system of your choice? What considerations are important when installing PyTorch, particularly in the context of GPU support?
3. Explain the concept of dynamic computation graphs in PyTorch. How does this dynamic nature benefit researchers and developers in deep learning projects?
4. What are tensors in PyTorch, and how do they differ from traditional data structures such as lists and arrays? Provide an example of how tensors are created and manipulated in PyTorch.
5. Discuss the advantages of GPU acceleration with PyTorch in deep learning applications. How does PyTorch seamlessly integrate with GPUs, and what considerations should be made when using GPUs for deep learning tasks?

6. Describe the steps involved in moving a PyTorch tensor to a GPU. How does this process contribute to faster computation in deep learning?
7. Compare Python versions (for example, Python 2.x and Python 3.x) in the context of PyTorch. Why is Python 3.x commonly recommended for PyTorch development?
8. Explain the core components of a Markov Decision Process (MDP). How are these components essential for modeling sequential decision-making problems in reinforcement learning?
9. Provide examples of typical operations that can be performed on PyTorch tensors. How are these tensor operations essential in the context of deep learning tasks?

Key Terms

- **PyTorch**: An open-source machine learning framework developed by Facebook's AI Research lab (FAIR), used for deep learning and neural network applications.
- **Dynamic Computation Graph**: A computational graph that is constructed dynamically during runtime, allowing for greater flexibility in defining and modifying neural network architectures.
- **Tensors**: Fundamental data structures in PyTorch, similar to NumPy arrays, used to store and manipulate multidimensional data.
- **GPU Acceleration**: The use of Graphics Processing Units (GPUs) to perform mathematical computations in parallel, significantly speeding up deep learning tasks.
- **Markov Decision Process (MDP)**: A mathematical framework used to model sequential decision-making problems, typically in the context of reinforcement learning. Components include states, actions, transition probabilities, and rewards.
- **NumPy**: A Python library for numerical operations, often used in conjunction with PyTorch for data manipulation.
- **Static Computation Graph**: A computational graph where the structure is defined before computation begins, in contrast to PyTorch's dynamic computation graph.
- **Data Types**: The specific data formats supported by PyTorch tensors, such as float, int, and others.
- **Element-Wise Operations**: Mathematical operations performed on corresponding elements of tensors, such as addition, subtraction, multiplication, and division.

CHAPTER 3
Text Preprocessing

Introduction

In the era of advancement in the field of Natural Language Processing (NLP), text data serves as the raw material on which the process of language understanding and machine intelligence is performed. Before we can begin on the journey of language modeling, sentiment analysis, or text classification, we must first lay the essential groundwork through a process known as "*Text Preprocessing*."

This chapter is related to the fundamental procedures that shape the foundation of NLP, where we transform unstructured text into structured text. Here, we will discuss text-related operations, such as tokenization, stop word removal, stemming, lemmatization, and the management of special characters and punctuation. These operations give way to the utilization of word embeddings such as Word2Vec, setting the stage for a deeper understanding of language and its application in the world of NLP.

Let us begin with the journey of text preprocessing, where we try to extract knowledge from the written word.

Structure

In this chapter, we will discuss the following topics:

- Tokenization
- Stop Word Removal
- Stemming and Lemmatization
- Handling Special Characters and Punctuation
- Word Embeddings and Word2Vec

Tokenization

Tokenization is the preliminary step in text preprocessing, where we break down raw text into smaller, meaningful units, typically words or subwords (*Figure 3.1*). These units are referred to as tokens. These tokens form the basis for various natural language processing tasks, allowing us to analyze and manipulate text data more effectively. Tokenization serves as the first bridge between the human language and the language understood by machines, making it a critical operation in any NLP pipeline.

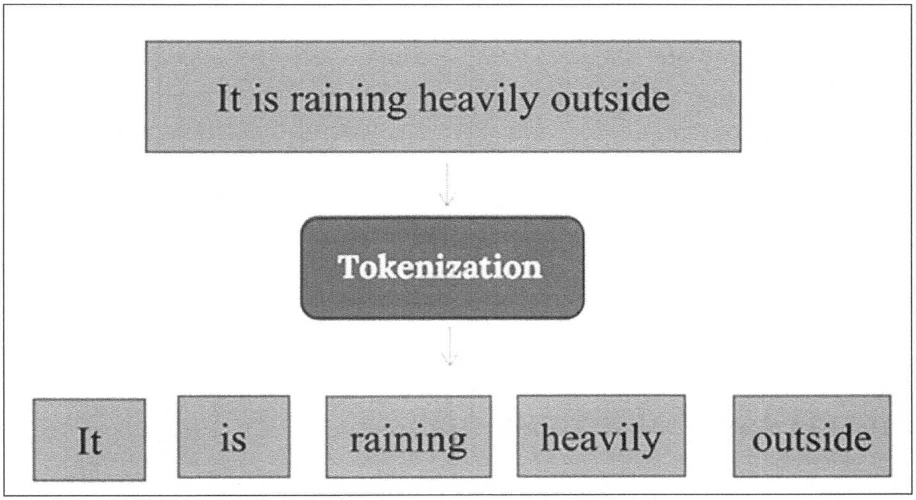

***Figure 3.1**: Tokenization*

The Tokenization Process

Tokenization is a crucial step in text preprocessing. It involves the following key steps:

- **Text Segmentation**: The process begins by segmenting the continuous stream of characters in a text document into individual chunks, which we call tokens. The most common approach is to split text in spaces, as this often corresponds to word boundaries in many languages. Tokenization is a language-dependent process, and languages with no clear word boundaries, namely Chinese or Japanese, require specialized techniques for performing tokenization.
- **Handling Special Cases**: Tokenization must also account for special cases, such as contractions ('*it's*'), hyphenated words ('*well-being*'), or abbreviations ('*Dr.*'). These cases may need to be treated as single tokens to ensure meaningful representation.
- **Normalization**: Tokens may require normalization to ensure consistency. This involves converting all text to lowercase to treat words in a case-insensitive manner.
- **Punctuation and Symbols**: Tokenization should also account for punctuation marks and symbols, as they often carry meaning.

Need for Tokenization

Let us explore the need for tokenization:

- **Granularity**: Tokenization allows us to work with text at a more granular level. This is crucial for many NLP tasks, as understanding the context of individual words is essential.
- **Text Processing Efficiency**: Once text is tokenized, we can easily count words, analyze word frequency, and perform operations such as stemming and lemmatization on individual tokens.
- **Statistical Analysis**: Tokenization enables the creation of a bag-of-words model, which is the foundation for various text analysis techniques, including document classification and sentiment analysis.
- **Language Models**: Modern language models rely on tokenized input. Tokenization is the first step in preparing text data for these powerful models.

Challenges in Tokenization

Tokenization is not without challenges, as it may involve different languages, domains, and text sources. Some of the common challenges include:

- **Ambiguity**: Words can have multiple meanings, and tokenization must consider the context to determine the appropriate tokenization.
- **Compound Words**: Some languages have long compound words that do not have spaces between them, making segmentation tricky.
- **Named Entities**: Regardless of spaces or punctuation, names of people, places, and organizations are often treated as single tokens.
- **Languages with No Spaces**: Some languages, such as Chinese, do not use spaces between words, making tokenization more complex.

Stop Word Removal

In the journey of text preprocessing for NLP, one important step that can significantly impact the quality and efficiency of our text data is the removal of **stop words**. Stop words are commonly used words in a language that add little semantic value to a sentence. They are words such as *the*, *and*, *in*, *is*, *of*, and so on. This is depicted in *Figure* 3.2. While they are essential for the structure of a language, they often do not carry much meaning in the context of specific NLP tasks.

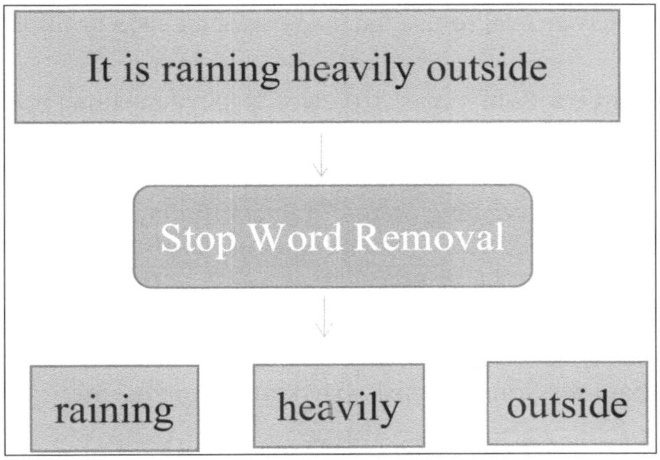

Figure 3.2: *Stop Word Removal*

Need for Stop Word Removal

Stop word removal is a vital process for several reasons:

- **Noise Reduction**: Removing stop words helps reduce noise in the text data. Noise in NLP refers to irrelevant information that can interfere with the analysis of meaningful content. By eliminating stop words, we focus on the more informative words that convey the core message.
- **Efficiency**: When performing tasks such as text classification or information retrieval, stop word removal can significantly improve the efficiency of algorithms. With fewer words to process, computational resources are used more effectively.
- **Improved Analytics**: The absence of stop words enhances the quality of text analytics. It allows for a clearer and more accurate representation of the significant words or phrases in a document, improving the effectiveness of techniques like term frequency analysis and document similarity measurements.
- **Storage and Memory**: For large text corpora, the removal of stop words can lead to a reduction in storage and memory requirements. This is especially important in scenarios with limited computational resources.

Challenges in Stop Word Removal

While removing stop words can be highly beneficial, there are some challenges and considerations to keep in mind:

- **Language-Dependent**: The list of stop words is language-dependent. What may be a stop word in one language could carry significant meaning in another.

Therefore, it is crucial to use language-specific lists or libraries to stop word removal.

- **Context Matters**: Sometimes, stop words carry meaning in specific contexts. For instance, the word "*not*" can be crucial in negation detection. To ensure context-specific meaning is not lost, take care while removing stop words.
- **Customization**: Depending on the NLP task, it may be necessary to customize the list of stop words. Some domain-specific stop words may need to be added to or removed from the standard list.
- **Lemmatization and Stemming**: If stemming or lemmatization is part of the preprocessing pipeline, it should be performed before stop word removal. This ensures that variations of words are treated consistently.

Implementing Stop Word Removal

Stop word removal can be implemented using readily available libraries and resources for various programming languages. Common libraries such as Natural Language Toolkit (NLTK) in Python provide predefined stop word lists for multiple languages. The process typically involves:

- Loading the list of stop words for the specific language.
- Tokenizing the text into words.
- Filtering out the stop words from the tokenized text.

Stop word removal is a critical step in text preprocessing for NLP, as it refines text data by eliminating words that add little to no meaning. This process contributes to improved data quality, efficiency, and the accuracy of subsequent NLP tasks, enabling more effective analysis and interpretation of textual information. However, it is essential to approach stop word removal with a consideration of language, context, and task-specific requirements to strike the right balance between noise reduction and information preservation.

Stemming and Lemmatization

Stemming and lemmatization are vital text preprocessing techniques in the realm of NLP that focus on transforming words into their base or root forms. The primary objective of these processes is to reduce inflected or derived words to a common form, making text data more manageable and enabling the recognition of shared semantics. While they serve a similar purpose, stemming and lemmatization differ in their approaches and precision.

Stemming

Stemming is the process of removing suffixes or prefixes from words to obtain the root form, known as the stem. Stemmers are heuristic algorithms designed to achieve this goal, and they do so by applying a series of transformation rules. The resulting stems may not always be real words, but they capture the core meaning of related words.

For instance, consider the words "*jumping*," "*jumps*," and "*jumped*." A stemming algorithm might reduce all of these words to the common stem "*jump*." This simplification allows NLP algorithms to treat these words as related, even though they have different forms.

Stemming algorithms are computationally efficient and work well for certain tasks, such as information retrieval and search engines. However, they can be overly aggressive, sometimes producing stems that are not actual words or failing to capture subtle differences in meaning.

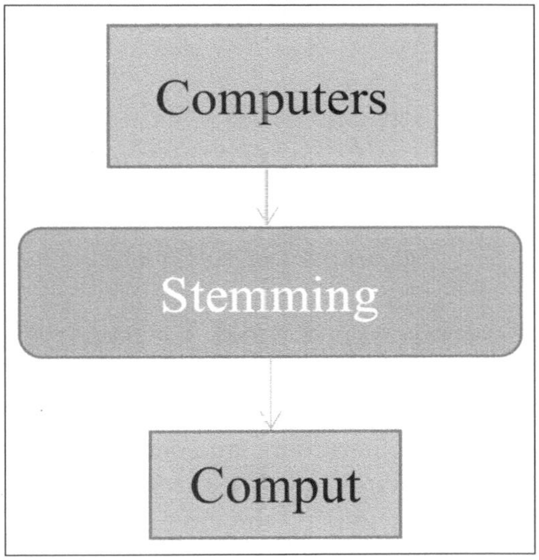

Figure 3.3: *Stemming*

Lemmatization

Lemmatization, on the other hand, is a more precise and linguistically informed process. It involves reducing words to their base or dictionary form, known as the lemma. Lemmatizers rely on linguistic knowledge and context to perform this transformation. The lemmatized forms are real words, preserving the semantic meaning of the word. This is depicted in *Figure* 3.4.

For example, in lemmatization, "*jumping*," "*jumps*," and "*jumped*" would all be lemmatized to "*jump*," the base form of the verb. This precision ensures that the transformed words remain grammatically correct and maintain their linguistic integrity.

Lemmatization is particularly useful in applications where the accuracy of word transformation is crucial, such as language generation, machine translation, or sentiment analysis. However, it is computationally more intensive and may not be as fast as stemming.

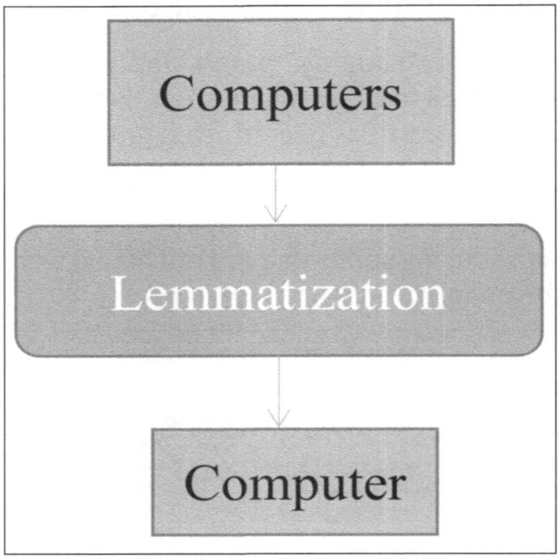

***Figure 3.4**: Lemmatization*

Challenges in Stemming and Lemmatization

Both stemming and lemmatization face challenges and limitations. These include:

- **Language Dependence**: Stemmers and lemmatizers are language-specific and require language-specific rules and resources. Different languages have unique linguistic features, making the development of these tools complex.
- **Contextual Ambiguity**: Sometimes, a word's meaning depends on the context. Stemming and lemmatization may not always capture contextual meaning accurately.
- **Over Stemming and Under Stemming**: Stemming can result in over stemming, where it reduces words too aggressively, or under stemming, where it retains unnecessary affixes. Lemmatization is less prone to these issues but is not entirely immune.
- **Part-of-Speech Consideration**: Lemmatization often requires part-of-speech information for accurate transformations. For example, "better" is a comparative adjective or adverb. Its lemma varies depending on the context and usage.

Implementing Stemming and Lemmatization

Stemming and lemmatization can be implemented using various libraries and tools, depending on the programming language and language-specific requirements. For example, the NLTK library in Python provides both stemming and lemmatization capabilities.

The general process involves:

- Tokenizing the text into words.
- Applying a stemming or lemmatization algorithm to each word.
- Obtaining the transformed or lemmatized words for further analysis.

Stemming and lemmatization are essential techniques in text preprocessing for NLP, as they aim to simplify word forms by reducing them to their base or root forms. While stemming is a faster, rule-based process, lemmatization is a more accurate and linguistically informed approach.

Handling Special Characters and Punctuation

In the field of NLP, the presence of special characters and punctuation marks within text data can introduce significant challenges. While special characters and punctuation often carry valuable information, they can also introduce noise and complexity into the text. In this section, we explore the importance of handling special characters and punctuation during text preprocessing and the methods for effectively managing them.

The Role of Special Characters and Punctuation

Special characters and punctuation marks are an integral part of written language. They serve various purposes, such as indicating sentence boundaries, separating clauses, conveying emotions, and expressing emphasis. Common examples include periods, commas, exclamation points, question marks, parentheses, quotation marks, and hyphens.

While these characters enhance the expressiveness and clarity of language, they can also hinder NLP tasks in the following ways:

- **Noise**: For some NLP applications, special characters and punctuation may introduce noise, making it challenging to focus on the core content of the text.
- **Tokenization**: Tokenization, the process of breaking text into individual words or tokens, can be complicated by punctuation. For instance, the sentence "*Dr. Smith is an M.D.*" includes periods that might interfere with correct tokenization.
- **Ambiguity**: Some punctuation marks, such as hyphens and apostrophes, can create ambiguity. For example, "*re-creation*" and "*recreation*" have different meanings, but without proper handling, they may be treated as the same word.

Methods for Handling Special Characters and Punctuation

Effectively managing special characters and punctuation is crucial for preparing text data for NLP tasks. Here are several methods to consider:

- **Removal**: In many cases, it is appropriate to remove certain special characters and punctuation marks. For example, removing most punctuation can simplify tokenization and reduce noise. However, it should be done judiciously to retain necessary information (for example, decimal points in numbers).
- **Replacement**: Some special characters can be replaced with their textual equivalents. For instance, replacing "&" with "*and*" or converting "*don't*" to "*do not*." This can improve tokenization and reduce ambiguity.
- **Preservation**: Certain punctuation marks, such as quotation marks and apostrophes, should be preserved as they can be crucial for understanding the text's meaning. Care should be taken to retain these marks during text preprocessing.
- **Contextual Handling**: In some cases, the decision to remove or preserve special characters should be based on the context. For instance, in sentiment analysis, emoticons or exclamation marks may carry valuable sentiment information and should not be removed.
- **Regular Expressions**: Regular expressions are powerful tools for pattern matching and can be used to selectively remove or replace specific characters or patterns in text data.

Challenges and Considerations

While managing special characters and punctuation, there are several challenges and considerations to keep in mind:

- **Language-Specific Rules**: The rules for handling special characters and punctuation can vary across languages. Some languages have unique punctuation marks and rules that may not be present in others.
- **Task-Specific Requirements**: The choice of how to handle special characters and punctuation should align with the specific NLP task. For example, sentiment analysis may require different handling than information retrieval.
- **Data Preservation**: Striking the right balance between noise reduction and information preservation is crucial. Overzealous removal of punctuation may result in the loss of valuable linguistic nuances.

Special characters and punctuation are a fundamental aspect of text data, and their appropriate handling during text preprocessing is critical for the success of NLP tasks. The choice of how to manage these elements depends on the specific task, language, and context. By implementing the right strategies, NLP practitioners can ensure that special characters and punctuation enhance, rather than hinder, the analysis and understanding of textual information.

Word Embeddings and Word2Vec

Word embeddings, particularly techniques such as Word2Vec, have revolutionized NLP by enabling machines to understand the meaning and context of words. In this section, we delve into the fascinating world of word embeddings, exploring how they transform raw text data into vector representations that capture semantic relationships and enhance the performance of NLP models.

Word Embeddings: The Essence of Vector Representations

In the field of NLP, words are fundamental building blocks, and understanding their meanings and context is essential. Traditional NLP methods used one-hot encoding to represent words as binary vectors, where each word was represented as a unique vector of zeros and a single '1' in the position corresponding to its index in the vocabulary. While this approach worked for some tasks, it ignored the semantic relationships between words. Word embeddings emerged as a solution to this problem.

Word embeddings are dense vector representations of words that capture semantic information based on their usage in context. Each word is mapped to a high-dimensional vector where similar words have vectors that are close in space, making it possible to capture meaning and relationships between words.

Word2Vec: A Breakthrough in Word Embeddings

One of the most influential techniques for creating word embeddings is Word2Vec, developed by Tomas Mikolov and his team at Google. Word2Vec employs a neural network architecture to learn word embeddings from large text corpora. It introduces two primary methods: Continuous Bag of Words (CBOW) and Skip-gram.

- **Continuous Bag of Words (CBOW)**: In CBOW, the model predicts the target word based on its surrounding context words. For example, given the context words "*The cat sat on the ____*," the model predicts the missing word "*mat*." CBOW is efficient and works well for smaller datasets.
- **Skip-gram**: Skip-gram predicts the context words given a target word. It is more suitable for large datasets and is better at capturing the relationships between words, including synonyms and antonyms. For example, given the

word "*king*," Skip-gram predicts "*man*," "*woman*," "*queen*," and so on, as its context.

CBOW is faster than Skip-gram. Also, Skip-gram is computationally more expensive.

Importance of Word2Vec

In NLP, Word2Vec has become conducive for several compelling reasons:

- **Semantic Meaning**: Word2Vec captures the semantic meaning of words by representing them as dense vectors. This enables NLP models to understand the relationships between words, such as "*king*" being related to "*queen*" and "*man*."
- **Vector Space Mathematics**: Once words are represented as vectors, you can perform vector operations to capture relationships. For example, the vector for "*king*" minus "*man*" plus "*woman*" yields a vector close to "*queen*."
- **Data Efficiency**: Word2Vec can learn meaningful embeddings from large text corpora, reducing the need for extensive feature engineering and manual rule-based techniques.
- **Transfer Learning**: Pre-trained Word2Vec embeddings can be used in downstream NLP tasks, saving time and resources. Many pre-trained word embeddings are available for various languages and domains.

Challenges and Considerations

Here are some challenges and considerations:

- **Size of Data**: Word2Vec benefits from large text corpora. Smaller datasets may not yield accurate embeddings.
- **Hyperparameter Tuning**: Parameters such as vector dimensionality, context window size, and training epochs must be chosen thoughtfully.
- **Domain Specificity**: Pre-trained Word2Vec embeddings may not capture domain-specific terminology. Fine-tuning on domain-specific data may be necessary.
- **Computational Resources**: Training Word2Vec models from scratch can be computationally expensive. Pre-trained models provide a valuable shortcut.

Word embeddings, especially techniques such as Word2Vec, have transformed NLP by providing a means to represent words as semantically meaningful vectors. These vectors capture the relationships between words, enabling NLP models to understand language in a more human-like manner. Word embeddings are a crucial tool for a wide range of NLP tasks, including text classification, sentiment analysis, and machine translation, and continue to drive innovation in the field.

Conclusion

In the field of Natural Language Processing (NLP), text preprocessing is the essential foundation upon which all language understanding and analysis tasks are built. This chapter has explored the critical techniques that form the core of text preprocessing: tokenization, stop word removal, stemming, lemmatization, and the handling of special characters and punctuation. Through these processes, we are able to bridge the gap between the intricacies of human language and the numerical representation required by machines to process, analyze, and understand text data.

Tokenization breaks the continuous stream of characters into meaningful units, enabling more granular analysis and facilitating language modeling. The removal of stop words eliminates the noise in our data, increasing computational efficiency and refining the quality of analytics. Stemming and lemmatization help us to extract semantic meanings and relationships between words. Word embeddings encapsulate the very essence of semantic meaning, transforming words into dense vectors that enable NLP models to comprehend relationships, context, and even perform vector space mathematics. By mastering the techniques in this chapter, you gain the power to unlock the hidden knowledge within textual data, enabling you to navigate the intricate nuances of language and harness its potential for a myriad of applications, from sentiment analysis to machine translation and beyond. The next chapter will explain how to build NLP models with PyTorch.

Points to Remember

- Tokenization is the process of breaking text into meaningful units, typically words or subwords.
- Stop words are common words that add little semantic value, such as "*the*," "*and*," "*in*," and "*is*."
- Removing stop words can reduce noise and enhance computational efficiency in NLP tasks.
- Stemming reduces words to their root form using heuristic algorithms, while lemmatization produces lemmas based on linguistic knowledge.
- Special characters and punctuation marks can carry valuable information but may also introduce noise.
- Word embeddings, such as Word2Vec, transform words into dense vectors that capture semantic meaning.
- Text preprocessing techniques are often language-dependent, and the choice of method should align with the language used in the text data.

Multiple Choice Questions

1. What is the primary purpose of tokenization in text preprocessing?
    a. To remove stop words
    b. To break text into meaningful units
    c. To perform stemming
    d. To handle special characters
2. Which of the following is a common example of a stop word?
    a. Running
    b. The
    c. Jumped
    d. Processing
3. Stemming and lemmatization are techniques used for:
    a. Tokenization
    b. Removing stop words
    c. Reducing words to their base or root form
    d. Handling special characters
4. What is the primary goal of stop word removal in text preprocessing?
    a. To increase computational efficiency
    b. To remove all punctuation marks
    c. To convert words to lowercase
    d. To capture semantic meaning
5. Which of the following is a challenge in stemming?
    a. Language independence
    b. Preserving all word variations
    c. Over stemming or under stemming
    d. Efficient computation
6. Special characters and punctuation can introduce which of the following into text data?
    a. Noise
    b. Semantic meaning
    c. Efficient tokenization
    d. Synonyms

7. What is the purpose of Word2Vec in NLP?
    a. To create stop word lists
    b. To perform text classification
    c. To transform words into dense vector representations
    d. To remove punctuation marks
8. Which Word2Vec method predicts the target word based on its surrounding context?
    a. Skip-gram
    b. CBOW
    c. Stemming
    d. Lemmatization
9. Which aspect of text preprocessing should be considered for language-dependent techniques?
    a. Overzealous removal
    b. Contextual handling
    c. Language and context dependence
    d. Data efficiency
10. What is the key benefit of pre-trained word embeddings, such as Word2Vec?
    a. They improve tokenization efficiency
    b. They eliminate the need for stop word removal
    c. They capture semantic meaning and can be used in various NLP tasks
    d. They preserve all punctuation marks

Answers

1. b
2. b
3. c
4. a
5. c
6. a
7. c

8. b
9. c
10. c

Questions

1. What is the primary objective of tokenization in text preprocessing, and how does it impact the analysis of text data?
2. Explain the concept of stop words and provide examples. Why is stop word removal considered an important step in text preprocessing?
3. Compare and contrast stemming and lemmatization in terms of their approaches and applications in NLP. Provide examples to illustrate the differences.
4. Discuss the challenges and limitations associated with stemming and lemmatization. How can these techniques handle languages with complex word forms?
5. Special characters and punctuation marks are integral to language, but they can also introduce noise into text data. Explain the methods for handling special characters and punctuation, highlighting the trade-off between information preservation and noise reduction.
6. Describe the significance of word embeddings in NLP and how they have transformed the field. How do word embeddings such as Word2Vec capture semantic meaning in textual data?
7. Explain the key methods employed by Word2Vec, specifically Continuous Bag of Words (CBOW) and Skip-gram. How do these methods differ in their approach to learning word embeddings?
8. When considering language-dependent techniques in text preprocessing, what factors should you take into account? How do these techniques adapt to various languages and domains?
9. Discuss the challenges and considerations associated with the efficient implementation of text preprocessing techniques. How can computational resources and pre-trained models be leveraged to streamline the process?
10. In the dynamic field of NLP, how can practitioners stay updated on the latest advancements in text preprocessing and adapt their methods to suit evolving requirements and challenges?

Key Terms

- **Tokenization**: Tokenization is the process of breaking text into smaller, meaningful units, often words or subwords. It serves as the foundational step in NLP, allowing text data to be analyzed at a more granular level.
- **Stop Words**: Stop words are common words in a language (for example, "*the*," "*and*," "*in*") that are often removed during text preprocessing to reduce noise and improve computational efficiency.
- **Stemming**: Stemming is a text normalization technique that reduces words to their base or root form by removing suffixes and prefixes. It is typically rule-based and aims to capture the core meaning of related words.
- **Lemmatization**: Lemmatization is a more precise text normalization process that reduces words to their base or dictionary form (lemma) using linguistic knowledge and context. Lemmatization ensures that the resulting words are real words.
- **Special Characters**: Special characters are non-alphabetic characters, symbols, or punctuation marks, such as "#," "@," or "&." They are commonly found in text data and require specific handling during preprocessing.
- **Punctuation Marks**: Punctuation marks are symbols used in written language to indicate sentence boundaries, convey emotions, or emphasize content. Examples include periods, commas, question marks, and exclamation points.
- **Word Embeddings**: Word embeddings are dense vector representations of words that capture their semantic meaning based on their context of use. Word embeddings enable NLP models to understand and work with words in a numerical format.
- **Word2Vec**: Word2Vec is a popular word embedding technique that uses neural networks to learn word embeddings from large text corpora. It offers two primary methods: Continuous Bag of Words (CBOW) and Skip-gram.
- **Information Preservation**: Information preservation in text preprocessing refers to the retention of meaningful and contextually important content while applying techniques to reduce noise and improve data quality. Striking a balance between noise reduction and information preservation is crucial.

CHAPTER 4
Building NLP Models with PyTorch

Introduction

In the field of Natural Language Processing (NLP), PyTorch has emerged as a powerful medium for researchers and practitioners. This chapter considers the practical aspects of building NLP models using the PyTorch framework. From fundamental tasks to advanced applications, we explore text processing using hands-on examples and fundamental insights.

The chapter begins with Text Classification, where we consider the techniques employed to categorize textual data. It includes Sentiment Analysis where we see how PyTorch facilitates the analysis of emotions and opinions within written content. Named Entity Recognition (NER) helps in guiding readers through the identification and extraction of entities such as names, locations, and organizations.

This chapter explains Part-of-Speech (POS) Tagging, a fundamental aspect of language understanding. It also explains Text Generation using Recurrent Neural Networks (RNNs), providing a glimpse of generating coherent and contextually relevant textual content.

Structure

In this chapter, we will discuss the following topics:

- Text Classification
- Sentiment Analysis
- Named Entity Recognition (NER)
- Part-of-Speech (POS) Tagging
- Machine Translation
- Text Generation with Recurrent Neural Networks (RNNs)

Text Classification

Text Classification is one of the important topics in Natural Language Processing, enabling machines to automatically categorize textual data into predefined classes or categories.

Text Classification involves training models to recognize patterns as well as features within text that help in assigning appropriate labels or categories to new, unseen text. Applications of Text Classification include spam detection, sentiment analysis, and topic categorization.

PyTorch, with its dynamic computational graph and user-friendly APIs, helps in providing an ideal environment for building text classification models. We will be using TorchText, which is an NLP-based library present in PyTorch, for performing NLP tasks. The Torch package can be used to define tensors.

Steps involved in text classification using PyTorch include the following:

First, install **`torchtext=0.6`** as follows:

```
pip install -U torchtext==0.6
```

1. **Import Libraries**

   ```
   import torch
   import torch.nn as nn
   import torch.optim as optim
   from torchtext import data, datasets
   ```

2. **Load and Preprocess the Data**

Define Tokenizer:

```
def simple_tokenizer(text):
    return text.split()
```

Load Dataset:

```
TEXT = data.Field(tokenize=simple_tokenizer)
LABEL = data.LabelField(dtype=torch.float)
train_data, test_data = datasets.IMDB.splits(TEXT, LABEL)
```

Build Vocabulary:

```
TEXT.build_vocab(train_data, max_size=25000, vectors="glove.6B.100d",
unk_init=torch.Tensor.normal_)
LABEL.build_vocab(train_data)
```

Create Data Iterators:

```
BATCH_SIZE = 64
device = torch.device('cuda' if torch.cuda.is_available() else 'cpu')
train_iterator, test_iterator = data.BucketIterator.splits(
```

```
    (train_data, test_data),
    batch_size=BATCH_SIZE,
    device=device,
    sort_key=lambda x: len(x.text),
    sort_within_batch=True
)
```

3. **Define the Model**

```
class SimpleNN(nn.Module):
    def __init__(self, input_dim, embedding_dim, hidden_dim, 
output_dim):
        super(SimpleNN, self).__init__()
        self.embedding = nn.Embedding(input_dim, embedding_dim)
        self.fc = nn.Linear(embedding_dim, hidden_dim)
        self.relu = nn.ReLU()
        self.out = nn.Linear(hidden_dim, output_dim)

    def forward(self, x):
        embedded = self.embedding(x)
        pooled = torch.mean(embedded, dim=1)
        hidden = self.relu(self.fc(pooled))
        output = self.out(hidden)
        return output
```

4. **Initialize Model, Loss Function, and Optimizer**

```
input_dim = len(TEXT.vocab)
embedding_dim = 100
hidden_dim = 256
output_dim = 1

model = SimpleNN(input_dim, embedding_dim, hidden_dim, output_
dim)

criterion = nn.BCEWithLogitsLoss()
optimizer = optim.Adam(model.parameters())
```

5. **Training Loop**

```
epochs = 5
for epoch in range(epochs):
    model.train()
    running_loss = 0.0

    for batch in train_iterator:
        text, labels = batch.text, batch.label
        optimizer.zero_grad()
        predictions = model(text).squeeze(1)
```

```
            loss = criterion(predictions, labels)
            loss.backward()
            optimizer.step()

            running_loss += loss.item()

        average_loss = running_loss / len(train_iterator)
        print(f'Epoch {epoch + 1}/{epochs}, Loss: {average_
loss:.4f}')
```

6. **Evaluation**

```
model.eval()
correct = 0
total = 0
with torch.no_grad():
    for batch in test_iterator:
        text, labels = batch.text, batch.label
        predictions = model(text).squeeze(1)
        predicted_labels = torch.round(torch.sigmoid(predictions))
        correct += (predicted_labels == labels).sum().item()
        total += labels.size(0)

accuracy = correct / totalprint(f'Test Accuracy: {accuracy *
100:.2f}%')
```

7. **Model Deployment (Optional)**

   Save the trained model for future use:

```
torch.save(model.state_dict(), 'text_classification_model.pth')

Load the model for inference:
loaded_model = SimpleNN(input_dim, embedding_dim, hidden_dim,
output_dim)
loaded_model.load_state_dict(torch.load('text_classification_
model.pth'))
loaded_model.eval()
```

These steps provide a basic outline for text classification using PyTorch. You can customize the model architecture, hyperparameters, and training procedure based on your specific requirements and dataset characteristics.

Sentiment Analysis

In this comprehensive exploration of Sentiment Analysis within the realm of natural language processing, we delve into the nuanced task of deciphering emotions and opinions from textual data, all powered by the robust capabilities of PyTorch.

Sentiment analysis holds immense significance, providing a lens through which we can understand the prevailing sentiments in various contexts, from customer reviews influencing business decisions to the pulse of social media during pivotal events.

Sentiment analysis, often referred to as opinion mining, involves determining the sentiment expressed in a piece of text. Here are the general steps for sentiment analysis using PyTorch:

First, install **`torchtext=0.6`** as follows:

```
pip install -U torchtext==0.6
```

1. **Import Libraries**

```
import torch
import torch.nn as nn
import torch.optim as optim
from torchtext import data, datasets
```

2. **Load and Preprocess the Data**

Define Tokenizer:

```
def simple_tokenizer(text):
    return text.split()
```

Load Dataset:

```
TEXT = data.Field(tokenize=simple_tokenizer)
LABEL = data.LabelField(dtype=torch.float)
train_data, test_data = datasets.IMDB.splits(TEXT, LABEL)
```

Build Vocabulary:

```
TEXT.build_vocab(train_data, max_size=25000, vectors="glove.6B.
100d", unk_init=torch.Tensor.normal_)
LABEL.build_vocab(train_data)
```

Create Data Iterators:

```
BATCH_SIZE = 64
device = torch.device('cuda' if torch.cuda.is_available() else
'cpu')

train_iterator, test_iterator = data.BucketIterator.splits(
    (train_data, test_data),
    batch_size=BATCH_SIZE,
    device=device,
    sort_key=lambda x: len(x.text),
    sort_within_batch=True
)
```

3. **Define the Sentiment Analysis Model**

```
class SentimentAnalysisNN(nn.Module):
    def __init__(self, input_dim, embedding_dim, hidden_dim,
output_dim):
        super(SentimentAnalysisNN, self).__init__()
        self.embedding = nn.Embedding(input_dim, embedding_dim)
        self.rnn = nn.LSTM(embedding_dim, hidden_dim,
bidirectional=True)
        self.fc = nn.Linear(hidden_dim * 2, output_dim)

    def forward(self, x):
        embedded = self.embedding(x)
        output, _ = self.rnn(embedded)
        avg_pool = torch.mean(output, dim=0)
        predictions = self.fc(avg_pool)
        return predictions
```

4. **Initialize Model, Loss Function, and Optimizer**

```
input_dim = len(TEXT.vocab)
embedding_dim = 100
hidden_dim = 256
output_dim = 1

model = SentimentAnalysisNN(input_dim, embedding_dim, hidden_dim,
output_dim)

criterion = nn.BCEWithLogitsLoss()
optimizer = optim.Adam(model.parameters())
```

5. **Training Loop**

```
epochs = 5
for epoch in range(epochs):
    model.train()
    running_loss = 0.0

    for batch in train_iterator:
        text, labels = batch.text, batch.label
        optimizer.zero_grad()
        predictions = model(text).squeeze(1)
        loss = criterion(predictions, labels)
        loss.backward()
        optimizer.step()

        running_loss += loss.item()
```

```
    average_loss = running_loss / len(train_iterator)
    print(f'Epoch {epoch + 1}/{epochs}, Loss: {average_
loss:.4f}')
```

6. **Evaluation**

```
model.eval()
correct = 0
total = 0
with torch.no_grad():
    for batch in test_iterator:
        text, labels = batch.text, batch.label
        predictions = model(text).squeeze(1)
        predicted_labels = torch.round(torch.sigmoid(predictions))
        correct += (predicted_labels == labels).sum().item()
        total += labels.size(0)

accuracy = correct / totalprint(f'Test Accuracy: {accuracy *
100:.2f}%')
```

7. **Model Deployment (Optional)**

```
Save the trained model for future use:
torch.save(model.state_dict(), 'sentiment_analysis_model.pth')
Load the Model for Inference:
loaded_model = SentimentAnalysisNN(input_dim, embedding_dim,
hidden_dim, output_dim)
loaded_model.load_state_dict(torch.load('sentiment_analysis_
model.pth'))
loaded_model.eval()
```

These steps provide a basic outline for sentiment analysis using PyTorch. Adjust the model architecture, hyperparameters, and training procedure based on your specific requirements and dataset characteristics.

Named Entity Recognition (NER)

Named Entity Recognition (NER), a pivotal task in natural language processing, takes the spotlight in this section as we delve into the intricacies of identifying and classifying entities within textual data using PyTorch. NER involves extracting and categorizing entities, such as names of people, locations, organizations, dates, and more, providing valuable information for information retrieval, question answering, and other NLP applications.

Understanding Named Entity Recognition

NER is a critical building block in language understanding, enabling systems to recognize and classify entities within text. By identifying and categorizing entities, NER contributes to a more nuanced comprehension of the semantics and structure of textual data.

NER is a task of extracting entities (such as names of persons, organizations, locations, and so on) from text. Here are the general steps for implementing NER using PyTorch:

First, install **`torchtext=0.6`** as follows:

```
pip install -U torchtext==0.6
```

1. **Import Libraries**

```
import torch
import torch.nn as nn
import torch.optim as optim
from torchtext import data, datasets
```

2. **Load and Preprocess the Data**

Define Tokenizer:

```
def simple_tokenizer(text):
    return text.split()
```

Load Dataset:

```
TEXT = data.Field(tokenize=simple_tokenizer)
ENTITY = data.Field()
fields = [('text', TEXT), ('entity', ENTITY)]
train_data, test_data = data.TabularDataset.splits(
    path='path/to/dataset',
    train='train.csv',
    test='test.csv',
    format='csv',
    fields=fields
)
```

Build Vocabulary:

```
TEXT.build_vocab(train_data, vectors="glove.6B.100d", unk_init=
torch.Tensor.normal_)
ENTITY.build_vocab(train_data)
```

Create Data Iterators:

```
BATCH_SIZE = 64
device = torch.device('cuda' if torch.cuda.is_available() else
'cpu')

train_iterator, test_iterator = data.BucketIterator.splits(
    (train_data, test_data),
```

```
        batch_size=BATCH_SIZE,
        device=device,
        sort_key=lambda x: len(x.text),
        sort_within_batch=True
    )
```

3. **Define the NER Model**

```
class NERModel(nn.Module):
    def __init__(self, input_dim, embedding_dim, hidden_dim,
output_dim):
        super(NERModel, self).__init__()
        self.embedding = nn.Embedding(input_dim, embedding_dim)
        self.rnn = nn.LSTM(embedding_dim, hidden_dim, bidirectional
=True)
        self.fc = nn.Linear(hidden_dim * 2, output_dim)

    def forward(self, x):
        embedded = self.embedding(x)
        output, _ = self.rnn(embedded)
        predictions = self.fc(output)
        return predictions
```

4. **Initialize Model, Loss Function, and Optimizer**

```
input_dim = len(TEXT.vocab)
embedding_dim = 100
hidden_dim = 256
output_dim = len(ENTITY.vocab)

model = NERModel(input_dim, embedding_dim, hidden_dim, output_dim)

criterion = nn.CrossEntropyLoss()
optimizer = optim.Adam(model.parameters())
```

5. **Training Loop**

```
epochs = 5
for epoch in range(epochs):
    model.train()
    running_loss = 0.0

    for batch in train_iterator:
        text, entity = batch.text, batch.entity
        optimizer.zero_grad()
        predictions = model(text)
        predictions = predictions.view(-1, predictions.shape[-1])
        entity = entity.view(-1)
        loss = criterion(predictions, entity)
        loss.backward()
```

```
            optimizer.step()
            running_loss += loss.item()

        average_loss = running_loss / len(train_iterator)
        print(f'Epoch {epoch + 1}/{epochs}, Loss: {average_
    loss:.4f}')
```

6. **Evaluation**

```
model.eval()
correct = 0
total = 0
with torch.no_grad():
    for batch in test_iterator:
        text, entity = batch.text, batch.entity
        predictions = model(text)
        predictions = predictions.view(-1, predictions.shape[-1])
        entity = entity.view(-1)
        _, predicted_entities = torch.max(predictions, 1)
        correct += (predicted_entities == entity).sum().item()
        total += entity.size(0)

accuracy = correct / totalprint(f'Test Accuracy: {accuracy *
100:.2f}%')
```

7. **Model Deployment (Optional)**

```
Save the trained model for future use:
torch.save(model.state_dict(), 'ner_model.pth')
Load the model for inference:
loaded_model = NERModel(input_dim, embedding_dim, hidden_dim,
output_dim)
loaded_model.load_state_dict(torch.load('ner_model.pth'))
loaded_model.eval()
```

These steps provide a basic outline for Named Entity Recognition (NER) using PyTorch. Customize the model architecture, hyperparameters, and training procedure based on your specific requirements and dataset characteristics.

Part-of-Speech (POS) Tagging

Part-of-speech tagging, a fundamental task in natural language processing, takes center stage in this section as we navigate the intricate landscape of linguistic analysis using PyTorch. POS tagging involves assigning a grammatical category, or part-of-speech, to each word in a given text, providing crucial syntactic information for downstream NLP tasks.

Here are the general steps for implementing POS tagging using PyTorch:

First, install **torchtext=0.6** as follows:

```
pip install -U torchtext==0.6
```

1. **Import Libraries**

```
import torch
import torch.nn as nn
import torch.optim as optim
from torchtext import data, datasets
```

2. **Load and Preprocess the Data**

Define Tokenizer:

```
def simple_tokenizer(text):
    return text.split()
```

Load Dataset:

```
TEXT = data.Field(tokenize=simple_tokenizer)
POS = data.Field()
fields = [('text', TEXT), ('pos', POS)]

train_data, test_data = data.TabularDataset.splits(
    path='path/to/dataset',
    train='train.csv',
    test='test.csv',
    format='csv',
    fields=fields
)
```

Build Vocabulary:

```
TEXT.build_vocab(train_data, vectors="glove.6B.100d", unk_init
=torch.Tensor.normal_)
POS.build_vocab(train_data)
```

Create Data Iterators:

```
BATCH_SIZE = 64
device = torch.device('cuda' if torch.cuda.is_available() else
'cpu')

train_iterator, test_iterator = data.BucketIterator.splits(
    (train_data, test_data),
    batch_size=BATCH_SIZE,
    device=device,
    sort_key=lambda x: len(x.text),
    sort_within_batch=True
)
```

3. **Define the POS Tagging Model**

```
class POSTagger(nn.Module):
    def __init__(self, input_dim, embedding_dim, hidden_dim,
output_dim):
        super(POSTagger, self).__init__()
        self.embedding = nn.Embedding(input_dim, embedding_dim)
        self.rnn = nn.LSTM(embedding_dim, hidden_dim, bidirectional
=True)
        self.fc = nn.Linear(hidden_dim * 2, output_dim)

    def forward(self, x):
        embedded = self.embedding(x)
        output, _ = self.rnn(embedded)
        predictions = self.fc(output)
        return predictions
```

4. **Initialize Model, Loss Function, and Optimizer**

```
input_dim = len(TEXT.vocab)
embedding_dim = 100
hidden_dim = 256
output_dim = len(POS.vocab)

model = POSTagger(input_dim, embedding_dim, hidden_dim, output_
dim)
criterion = nn.CrossEntropyLoss()
optimizer = optim.Adam(model.parameters())
```

5. **Training Loop**

```
epochs = 5
for epoch in range(epochs):
    model.train()
    running_loss = 0.0

    for batch in train_iterator:
        text, pos = batch.text, batch.pos
        optimizer.zero_grad()
        predictions = model(text)
        predictions = predictions.view(-1, predictions.shape[-1])
        pos = pos.view(-1)
        loss = criterion(precictions, pos)
        loss.backward()
        optimizer.step()

        running_loss += loss.item()
```

```
    average_loss = running_loss / len(train_iterator)
    print(f'Epoch {epoch + 1}/{epochs}, Loss: {average_
loss:.4f}')
```

6. **Evaluation**

```
model.eval()
correct = 0
total = 0
with torch.no_grad():
    for batch in test_iterator:
        text, pos = batch.text, batch.pos
        predictions = model(text)
        predictions = predictions.view(-1, predictions.shape[-1])
        pos = pos.view(-1)
        _, predicted_pos = torch.max(predictions, 1)
        correct += (predicted_pos == pos).sum().item()
        total += pos.size(0)

accuracy = correct / totalprint(f'Test Accuracy: {accuracy *
100:.2f}%')
```

7. **Model Deployment (Optional)**

   Save the trained model for future use:

```
torch.save(model.state_dict(), 'pos_tagging_model.pth')
```

   Load the Model for Inference:

```
loaded_model = POSTagger(input_dim, embedding_dim, hidden_dim,
output_dim)
loaded_model.load_state_dict(torch.load('pos_tagging_model.pth'))
loaded_model.eval()
```

These steps provide a basic outline for Part-of-Speech (POS) tagging using PyTorch. Customize the model architecture, hyperparameters, and training procedure based on your specific requirements and dataset characteristics.

Machine Translation

Machine Translation (MT), a transformative application of natural language processing, comes to the forefront in this section as we explore the mechanisms and methodologies behind translating text from one language to another using PyTorch 2.0. Machine Translation plays a pivotal role in breaking down language barriers and facilitating cross-cultural communication by automating the process of rendering text in different languages.

Understanding Machine Translation

Machine Translation involves the use of computational models to automatically translate text from a source language to a target language. The task is multifaceted, encompassing the challenges of capturing linguistic nuances, idiomatic expressions, and context-specific meanings.

Here are the general steps for implementing machine translation using PyTorch:

First install **`torchtext=0.6`** as follows:

```
pip install -U torchtext==0.6
```

1. **Import Libraries**

```
import torch
import torch.nn as nn
import torch.optim as optim
from torchtext import data, datasets
```

2. **Load and Preprocess the Data**

   Define Tokenizers:

```
def tokenize_source(text):
    return text.split()
def tokenize_target(text):
    return text.split()
```

   Load Dataset:

```
SRC = data.Field(tokenize=tokenize_source, init_token='<sos>',
eos_token='<eos>', lower=True)
TRG = data.Field(tokenize=tokenize_target, init_token='<sos>',
eos_token='<eos>', lower=True)

train_data, validation_data, test_data = datasets.Multi30k.
splits(
    exts=('.de', '.en'),
    fields=(SRC, TRG)
)
```

   Build Vocabulary:

```
SRC.build_vocab(train_data, min_freq=2)
TRG.build_vocab(train_data, min_freq=2)
```

   Create Data Iterators:

```
BATCH_SIZE = 64
device = torch.device('cuda' if torch.cuda.is_available() else
'cpu')
```

```
train_iterator, valid_iterator, test_iterator = data.Bucket
Iterator.splits(
    (train_data, validation_data, test_data),
    batch_size=BATCH_SIZE,
    device=device
)
```

3. **Define the Machine Translation Model**

```
class Seq2Seq(nn.Module):
    def __init__(self, encoder, decoder, device):
        super(Seq2Seq, self).__init__()
        self.encoder = encoder
        self.decoder = decoder
        self.device = device

    def forward(self, src, trg, teacher_forcing_ratio=0.5):
        # Implementation of the forward pass
        pass
```

4. **Initialize Model, Loss Function, and Optimizer**

```
INPUT_DIM = len(SRC.vocab)
OUTPUT_DIM = len(TRG.vocab)
ENC_EMB_DIM = 256
DEC_EMB_DIM = 256
HID_DIM = 512
N_LAYERS = 2
ENC_DROPOUT = 0.5
DEC_DROPOUT = 0.5

enc = Encoder(INPUT_DIM, ENC_EMB_DIM, HID_DIM, N_LAYERS, ENC_
DROPOUT)
dec = Decoder(OUTPUT_DIM, DEC_EMB_DIM, HID_DIM, N_LAYERS, DEC_
DROPOUT)

model = Seq2Seq(enc, dec, device)

criterion = nn.CrossEntropyLoss(ignore_index=TRG.vocab.
stoi['<pad>'])
optimizer = optim.Adam(model.parameters())
```

5. **Training Loop**

```
epochs = 10
for epoch in range(epochs):
    model.train()
    running_loss = 0.0
```

```
    for batch in train_iterator:
        src, trg = batch.src, batch.trg
        optimizer.zero_grad()
        output = model(src, trg)
        output_dim = output.shape[-1]
        output = output[1:].view(-1, output_dim)
        trg = trg[1:].view(-1)
        loss = criterion(output, trg)
        loss.backward()
        optimizer.step()

        running_loss += loss.item()

    average_loss = running_loss / len(train_iterator)
    print(f'Epoch {epoch + 1}/{epochs}, Loss: {average_
loss:.4f}')
```

6. **Evaluation**

```
model.eval()# Implement the evaluation loop
```

7. **Model Deployment (Optional)**

   Save the Trained Model for Future Use:

```
torch.save(model.state_dict(), 'machine_translation_model.pth')

Load the model for inference:
loaded_model = Seq2Seq(enc, dec, device)
loaded_model.load_state_dict(torch.load('machine_translation_
model.pth'))
loaded_model.eval()
```

These steps provide a basic outline for machine translation using PyTorch. One can customize the model architecture, hyperparameters, and training procedure based on the specific requirements and dataset characteristics.

Text Generation with RNNs

Text generation stands as a captivating endeavor within the realm of natural language processing, and in this section, we focus on the application of Recurrent Neural Networks (RNNs) to generate coherent and contextually relevant textual content. Text generation has diverse applications, from creative writing and storytelling to the automated production of human-like language for chatbots and virtual assistants.

Text generation involves the creation of new sequences of words or characters that follow a given pattern or style. In the context of natural language processing, text generation often entails producing human-like language that maintains semantic coherence and grammatical structure. This section explores the principles behind text generation and its role in various creative and practical applications.

Recurrent Neural Networks for Text Generation

RNNs, a class of neural networks designed to work with sequential data, prove particularly effective in capturing the dependencies and contextual information inherent in language. Their ability to maintain a hidden state that retains information from previously used steps makes them well-suited for tasks such as text generation.

Text generation using RNN involves the following steps:

1. **Importing Libraries**

```
import torch
import torch.nn as nn
import torch.optim as optim
```

2. **Define the SimpleRNN Model**

```
class SimpleRNN(nn.Module):
    def __init__(self, input_size, hidden_size, output_size):
        super(SimpleRNN, self).__init__()
        self.embedding = nn.Embedding(input_size, hidden_size)
        self.rnn = nn.RNN(hidden_size, hidden_size)
        self.fc = nn.Linear(hidden_size, output_size)

    def forward(self, x, hidden):
        embedded = self.embedding(x)
        output, hidden = self.rnn(embedded, hidden)
        output = self.fc(output)
        return output, hidden
```

This defines a simple RNN model with an embedding layer, an RNN layer, and a fully connected layer. The forward method describes how data flows through the model.

3. **Function to Generate Text**

```
def generate_text(model, seed_text, length=50):
    model.eval()
    with torch.no_grad():
        seed = torch.LongTensor([word_to_index[word] for word in
seed_text.split()]).unsqueeze(1)
        hidden = torch.zeros(1, 1, hidden_size)
        generated_text = seed_text

        for _ in range(length):
```

```
            output, hidden = model(seed, hidden)
            predicted_index = torch.argmax(output[-1]).item()
            predicted_word = index_to_word[predicted_index]
            generated_text += ' ' + predicted_word
            seed = torch.LongTensor([[predicted_index]])
    return generated_text
```

This function takes a trained model, a seed text, and generates new text by predicting the next word in a loop.

4. **Sample Data and Preprocessing**

```
data = "Hello world, how are you doing today? This is a sample
text for training an RNN."
words = data.split()
word_to_index = {word: idx for idx, word in enumerate(set(words))}
index_to_word = {idx: word for idx, word in enumerate(set(words))}
input_size = len(word_to_index)
hidden_size = 128
output_size = len(word_to_index)
```

This is a simple example dataset and basic preprocessing. It tokenizes the input text into words and creates mappings between words and indices.

5. **Model Initialization, Loss Function, and Optimizer**

```
model = SimpleRNN(input_size, hidden_size, output_size)
criterion = nn.CrossEntropyLoss()
optimizer = optim.Adam(model.parameters(), lr=0.001)
Here, we initialize the model, set up the loss function
(CrossEntropyLoss), and use the Adam optimizer.
```

6. **Training Loop**

```
epochs = 100for epoch in range(epochs):
    model.train()
    optimizer.zero_grad()

    input_sequence = torch.LongTensor([word_to_index[word] for
word in words[:-1]])
    target_sequence = torch.LongTensor([word_to_index[word] for
word in words[1:]])

    hidden = torch.zeros(1, 1, hidden_size)
    output, _ = model(input_sequence.unsqueeze(1), hidden)

    loss = criterion(output.view(-1, output_size), target_sequence)
    loss.backward()
    optimizer.step()
```

```
        if (epoch + 1) % 10 == 0:
            generated_text = generate_text(model, seed_text="Hello", 
length=20)
            print(f'Epoch {epoch + 1}/{epochs}, Loss: {loss.
item():.4f}, Generated Text: {generated_text}')
```

This is the training loop where the model is trained to predict the next word in the sequence. Every 10 epochs, it generates some text using the `generate_text` function to check the progress.

This is a very basic example, and for real-world scenarios, you may want to use more complex models and larger datasets.

Conclusion

In this chapter, we have discussed many natural language processing tasks along with their implementation and techniques. From foundational tasks such as Text Classification, Sentiment Analysis, Named Entity Recognition, and Part-of-Speech Tagging, to more advanced applications such as Machine Translation and Text Generation with Recurrent Neural Networks, we have witnessed the versatility and power of PyTorch in addressing the complexities of language understanding.

We have discussed data preparation and preprocessing, understanding the importance of clean and well-structured datasets.

Real-world applications highlighted the tangible impact of NLP models across various domains, from business and marketing to healthcare and communication. Creative examples in text generation illustrated the potential for AI to contribute to the realms of literature, creative writing, and human-like language production.

Moving ahead, we glimpsed into the future trends and challenges within the field of NLP, recognizing the evolving nature of language processing tasks and the ongoing role of PyTorch in shaping the landscape.

As we conclude this chapter, readers are equipped with a holistic understanding of building NLP models with PyTorch. Whether embarking on sentiment analysis, extracting named entities, or generating creative text, the principles and practical insights gained here serve as a solid foundation for further exploration and innovation in the dynamic field of natural language processing. In the next chapter, we will delve into the realm of Advanced NLP Techniques with PyTorch.

Points to Remember

- Text Classification involves categorizing textual data into predefined classes.
- Sentiment Analysis involves analyzing and categorizing emotions and opinions within text.

- Real-world applications of Sentiment Analysis include customer feedback analysis and social media sentiment monitoring.
- Named Entity Recognition is recognition and classification of Named Entities in a text.
- Applications of NER range from information retrieval to biomedical text analysis.
- POS Tagging involves assigning part of speech or grammatical categories to words in a sentence.
- Machine Translation involves the translation of text from one language to another using computational models.

Multiple Choice Questions

1. What is the primary role of Named Entity Recognition (NER) in natural language processing?
   a. Identifying sentiment in text
   b. Categorizing entities such as names and locations
   c. Translating text between languages
   d. Analyzing part-of-speech in sentences
2. Which PyTorch feature makes it suitable for dynamic neural network construction in NLP?
   a. Static computational graph
   b. Fixed model architecture
   c. Dynamic computational graph
   d. Limited flexibility
3. What is the primary purpose of Part-of-Speech (POS) tagging in NLP?
   a. Identifying entities in text
   b. Analyzing sentiment in sentences
   c. Assigning grammatical categories to words
   d. Translating text between languages

4. Which type of neural network architecture is commonly used for Named Entity Recognition (NER)?
   a. Convolutional Neural Network (CNN)
   b. Recurrent Neural Network (RNN)
   c. Long Short-Term Memory (LSTM)
   d. Decision Tree
5. What is the primary function of the attention mechanism in machine translation models?
   a. Handling data preprocessing
   b. Identifying and focusing on relevant parts of the input sequence
   c. Defining loss functions for training
   d. Evaluating translation quality
6. Which task involves automatically categorizing textual data into predefined classes?
   a. Named Entity Recognition
   b. Sentiment Analysis
   c. Machine Translation
   d. Text Generation
7. What is the role of transfer learning in natural language processing?
   a. Initializing models with random weights
   b. Training models from scratch for each task
   c. Leveraging pretrained models and embeddings
   d. Ignoring pre-existing linguistic knowledge
8. Which PyTorch component facilitates the creation of machine translation models?
   a. Static computational graph
   b. Dynamic computational graph
   c. Fixed model architecture
   d. Limited flexibility

9. What is a crucial consideration when working with real-world applications of NLP models?
    a. Ignoring user feedback
    b. Prioritizing model complexity over interpretability
    c. Disregarding ethical considerations
    d. Considering scalability and user experience
10. In text generation with Recurrent Neural Networks (RNNs), what does the hidden state retain across time steps?
    a. Previous input data
    b. Gradient values during backpropagation
    c. Information from previous time steps
    d. Future input data

Answers

1. b
2. c
3. c
4. c
5. b
6. b
7. c
8. b
9. d
10. c

Questions

1. How does text classification differ from sentiment analysis, and what are the key applications of text classification in NLP?
2. Explain the importance of sentiment analysis in business decision-making and provide an example of a real-world scenario where sentiment analysis could be beneficial.

3. What challenges are associated with named entity recognition, and how can PyTorch 2.0's features address these challenges in NER model development?
4. Elaborate on the significance of part-of-speech tagging in language understanding and provide an example of how POS tagging can enhance NLP applications.
5. How does the dynamic nature of PyTorch 2.0 contribute to the effectiveness of recurrent neural networks in text generation, and what are the potential challenges in generating coherent and contextually relevant text?
6. Identify and discuss one emerging trend and one potential challenge in the field of NLP, considering the evolving landscape and the role of PyTorch 2.0 in addressing these trends and challenges.
7. Explain the challenges related to scalability when working with large datasets in NLP. Additionally, discuss different deployment strategies for NLP models in real-world applications.

Key Terms

- **Text Classification**: The task of categorizing textual data into predefined classes, providing a foundation for various natural language processing applications.
- **Sentiment Analysis**: The process of analyzing and categorizing the emotional tone or opinion expressed in text, often categorized as positive, negative, or neutral sentiments.
- **Named Entity Recognition (NER)**: The task of identifying and classifying named entities, such as names of people, locations, organizations, and dates, within a given text.
- **Part-of-Speech (POS) Tagging**: The process of assigning grammatical categories, or parts of speech, to each word in a sentence, aiding in syntactic and grammatical analysis.
- **Machine Translation**: The automated process of translating text from one language to another using computational models, facilitating cross-language communication.
- **Text Generation**: The task of creating new textual content, often using neural networks, with applications in creative writing, storytelling, and chatbot responses.
- **Recurrent Neural Networks (RNNs)**: A type of neural network designed to work with sequential data, where the hidden state retains information from previously used steps, making it suitable for tasks like text generation.

- **Dynamic Computational Graph**: A computational graph that is constructed on-the-fly during model execution, allowing for flexibility and adaptability in PyTorch 2.0.
- **Data Preprocessing**: The process of preparing raw data for model training, including techniques such as tokenization, embedding representation, and handling of sequential data.
- **Attention Mechanism**: A component in neural network architectures, often used in machine translation, that allows the model to focus on specific parts of the input sequence during processing.
- **Transfer Learning**: A machine learning paradigm where pre-trained models or knowledge are leveraged to improve the performance of models on a specific task.
- **Hyperparameter Tuning**: The process of adjusting hyperparameters, such as learning rates and batch sizes, to optimize the performance of a machine learning model.

CHAPTER 5
Advanced NLP Techniques with PyTorch

Introduction

There have been remarkable advancements in the field of Natural Language Processing (NLP) in recent years fueled by the synergy between cutting-edge techniques and powerful computational frameworks such as PyTorch. In this chapter, we delve into the realm of Advanced NLP Techniques with PyTorch, exploring methodologies that have revolutionized the way machines understand and generate human language.

We begin our journey by discovering the intricacies of Sequence-to-Sequence Models. These models have gained widespread popularity for their efficacy in various NLP tasks such as machine translation, text summarization, and conversational agents. Through PyTorch's flexible architecture, we navigate the implementation of sequence-to-sequence models, understanding their underlying mechanisms and optimizing their performance.

Attention Mechanisms emerge as a pivotal innovation in the domain of NLP, enabling models to focus on relevant parts of input sequences during processing. We will discuss the conceptual framework of attention mechanisms and demonstrate their implementation in PyTorch, showcasing how they enhance the capabilities of neural networks in tasks demanding contextual understanding and information extraction.

The advent of Transformer Models marks a paradigm shift in NLP, offering unparalleled efficiency and scalability in modeling long-range dependencies within sequences.

Transfer Learning emerges as a potent technique for leveraging pre-trained models to bootstrap NLP tasks with limited labeled data. We explore transfer learning strategies tailored for NLP tasks using PyTorch, empowering practitioners to harness the wealth of knowledge encoded within pre-trained language representations effectively.

Finally, we will discuss Language Modeling with GPT-3.5, a state-of-the-art generative model that exemplifies the prowess of large-scale language models. Through PyTorch's seamless integration with GPT-3.5, we uncover the intricacies of language modeling and explore innovative applications, from text generation to natural language understanding tasks.

Structure

In this chapter, we will discuss the following topics:

- Sequence-to-Sequence Models
- Attention Mechanisms
- Transformer Models
- Transfer Learning for NLP
- Language Modeling with GPT-3.5

Sequence-to-Sequence Models

Sequence-to-Sequence (Seq2Seq) models represent a fundamental paradigm in Natural Language Processing (NLP), revolutionizing tasks such as machine translation, text summarization, and conversational agents. At its core, Seq2Seq architecture comprises an encoder-decoder framework, where an input sequence is encoded into a fixed-length vector representation by the encoder, which is subsequently decoded into an output sequence by the decoder.

The encoder processes the input sequence, typically a sequence of words or tokens, into a hidden state vector that captures the contextual information of the entire input. This hidden state acts as a summary of the input sequence, condensing the relevant information into a fixed-size representation. Various recurrent neural network (RNN) architectures, such as Long Short-Term Memory (LSTM) or Gated Recurrent Unit (GRU), have traditionally been employed as encoders due to their ability to capture sequential dependencies effectively.

Once the input sequence is encoded, the decoder utilizes this hidden state to generate the output sequence one token at a time. At each step, the decoder attends to the encoded input sequence, focusing on different parts of the input depending on the current context. This attention mechanism enables the model to align input and output sequences appropriately, facilitating accurate sequence generation.

Seq2Seq models have demonstrated remarkable success in diverse NLP tasks. In machine translation, they excel at translating text from one language to another by encoding the source language into a vector representation and decoding it into the target language. Similarly, in text summarization, they condense lengthy documents into concise summaries by encoding the input text and generating a summary sequence. Additionally, Seq2Seq models power conversational agents, allowing them to understand user inputs and generate coherent responses.

PyTorch provides a robust framework for implementing Seq2Seq models, offering flexibility in designing custom architectures and efficient computation through its dynamic computation graph. By leveraging PyTorch's capabilities, practitioners can develop sophisticated Seq2Seq models tailored to specific NLP tasks, fine-tuning architectures and hyperparameters to achieve optimal performance. *Figure 5.1* shows the use of a sequence-to-sequence model. It may be used for performing Machine Translation, Text Summarization, and so on.

Sequence-to-Sequence models involve the following:

- **Architecture Variants**: While the basic Seq2Seq architecture employs recurrent neural networks (RNNs) such as LSTM or GRU as both the encoder and decoder, variations have emerged to address limitations such as vanishing gradients and the inability to capture long-range dependencies effectively. One popular variant is the use of bidirectional RNNs in the encoder, allowing it to consider both past and future context when generating the hidden state. Additionally, attention mechanisms have become a standard component in Seq2Seq models, enabling more flexible and accurate alignment between input and output sequences.

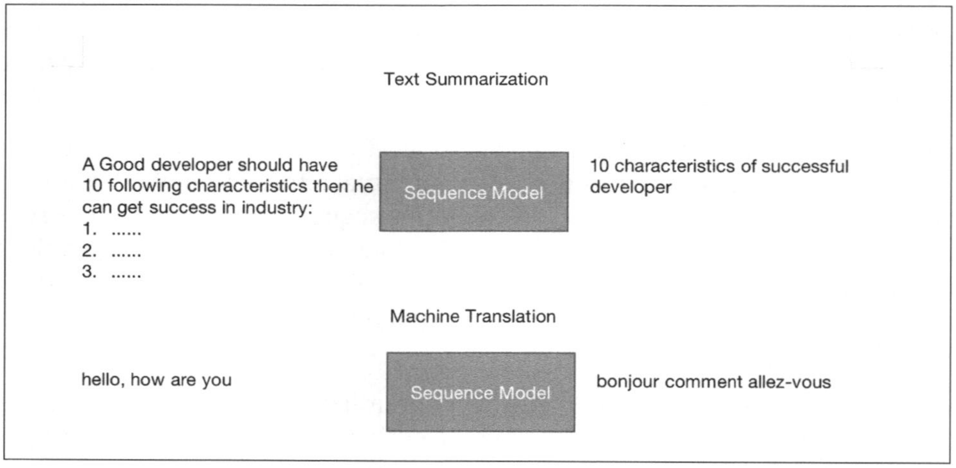

***Figure 5.1**: Use of Sequence-to-Sequence Model*

- **Training Dynamics**: Training Seq2Seq models involves optimizing parameters to minimize a suitable loss function, typically cross-entropy loss for sequence generation tasks. The training process involves feeding the input sequence into the encoder, generating the hidden state, and then using it to initialize the decoder. During decoding, the model iteratively predicts the next token in the output sequence until an end-of-sequence token is generated or a maximum length is reached. The parameters of both the encoder and decoder are updated using backpropagation through time (BPTT), which unfolds the computation graph over the entire sequence.

- **Beam Search and Decoding Strategies**: While greedy decoding is straightforward, it may lead to suboptimal sequences due to its myopic nature. Beam search is a popular decoding strategy that explores multiple candidate sequences in parallel, maintaining a fixed number of top sequences (known as the beam width) at each step. This approach allows the model to consider a wider range of possibilities and often leads to better-quality output sequences. Other decoding strategies include sampling-based methods such as stochastic decoding and diverse decoding, which introduce randomness to explore the solution space more comprehensively.
- **Handling Variable-Length Sequences**: One challenge in Seq2Seq modeling is handling variable-length input and output sequences. While padding can be used to ensure fixed-length input sequences, it may introduce unnecessary computation and memory overhead. Alternatively, techniques such as packing and unpacking sequences allow the model to process variable-length sequences efficiently by dynamically adjusting the computation graph. Attention mechanisms play a crucial role in addressing this challenge, enabling the model to focus on relevant parts of the input sequence during decoding regardless of its length.
- **Applications and Extensions**: Seq2Seq models have found applications beyond traditional tasks such as machine translation and text summarization. They are increasingly used in tasks such as image captioning, where they generate natural language descriptions of images, and speech recognition, where they convert audio input into text. Moreover, extensions such as conditional Seq2Seq models, which condition the generation process on additional input information, have enabled more sophisticated applications such as style transfer and text-based image generation.

Attention Mechanisms

Attention mechanisms have emerged as a cornerstone in modern Natural Language Processing (NLP), revolutionizing the way neural networks process sequential data. Originally introduced to address limitations in sequence-to-sequence (Seq2Seq) models, attention mechanisms enable models to focus on relevant parts of the input sequence during processing, dynamically adjusting their attention based on the context of the task.

At its essence, an attention mechanism allows a model to assign different weights to different parts of the input sequence, indicating their relative importance in generating the output sequence. This stands in contrast to traditional Seq2Seq models, where the entire input sequence is encoded into a fixed-length representation, potentially leading to information loss or ambiguity, especially in long sequences.

The key components of an attention mechanism include:

- **Query, Key, and Value**: These are three vectors derived from the input sequence, each serving a distinct purpose in the attention computation. The query vector represents the current state of the decoder, indicating what information is being sought from the input. The key vector captures information from the input sequence, while the value vector represents the actual content of the input sequence.
- **Attention Scores**: Attention scores quantify the relevance of each element in the input sequence with respect to the current state of the decoder. These scores are computed using a similarity function, such as dot product, scaled dot product, or concatenation followed by a neural network layer. Higher scores indicate higher relevance, guiding the model's focus during decoding.
- **Attention Weights**: Attention scores are typically transformed into attention weights through a SoftMax operation, ensuring that the weights sum up to one and represent a valid probability distribution over the input sequence. These weights determine how much attention each element in the input sequence receives during decoding.
- **Context Vector**: The weighted sum of the value vectors, each weighted by its corresponding attention weight, forms the context vector. This context vector encapsulates the relevant information from the input sequence, providing additional context to the decoder for generating the output sequence.

Attention mechanisms offer several advantages in NLP tasks:

- **Improved Model Performance**: By focusing on relevant parts of the input sequence, attention mechanisms enable models to capture long-range dependencies and intricate patterns more effectively, leading to improved performance in tasks such as machine translation, text summarization, and sentiment analysis. *Figure 5.2* shows the use of the Attention Mechanism in Sentiment Analysis.
- **Interpretability**: Attention mechanisms provide insights into the inner workings of the model, highlighting which parts of the input sequence contribute most to the generation of specific output tokens. This interpretability enhances trust and understanding of model predictions, crucial for applications in sensitive domains such as healthcare and finance.
- **Handling Variable-Length Sequences**: Attention mechanisms naturally accommodate variable-length input sequences, as they dynamically adjust their attention based on the length and content of the input. This flexibility makes attention-based models more robust and scalable across different tasks and datasets.

Task: Hotel location

you get what you pay for . not the cleanest rooms but bed was clean and so was bathroom . bring your own towels though as very thin . service was excellent , let us book in at 8:30am ! **for location and price , this ca n't be beaten ,** but it is cheap for a reason . if you come expecting the hilton , then book the hilton ! for uk travellers , think of a blackpool b&b.

Task: Hotel cleanliness

you get what you pay for . **not the cleanest rooms but bed was clean and so was bathroom** . bring your own towels though as very thin . service was excellent , let us book in at 8:30am ! for location and price , this ca n't be beaten , but it is cheap for a reason . if you come expecting the hilton , then book the hilton ! for uk travellers , think of a blackpool b&b.

Task: Hotel service

you get what you pay for . not the cleanest rooms but bed was clean and so was bathroom . bring your own towels though as very thin . **service was excellent ,** let us book in at 8:30am ! for location and price , this ca n't be beaten , but it is cheap for a reason . if you come expecting the hilton , then book the hilton ! for uk travellers , think of a blackpool b&b.

Figure 5.2: *Attention Mechanism for Aspect-based Sentiment Analysis (from Y. Bao, S. Chang, M. Yu, and R. Barzilay, "Deriving machine attention from human rationales," in Proc. EMNLP, 2018, pp. 1903–1913). Words in bold have maximum attention score and are considered relevant for sentiment analysis*

Transformer Models

Transformer models have emerged as a groundbreaking architecture in the field of NLP. introducing a novel approach to capturing long-range dependencies within sequential data. It is shown in *Figure 5.3*. Proposed in the seminal paper "*Attention is All You Need*" by *Vaswani et al.* in 2017, transformers have since become the de facto standard for a wide range of NLP tasks, surpassing previous architectures in both performance and efficiency.

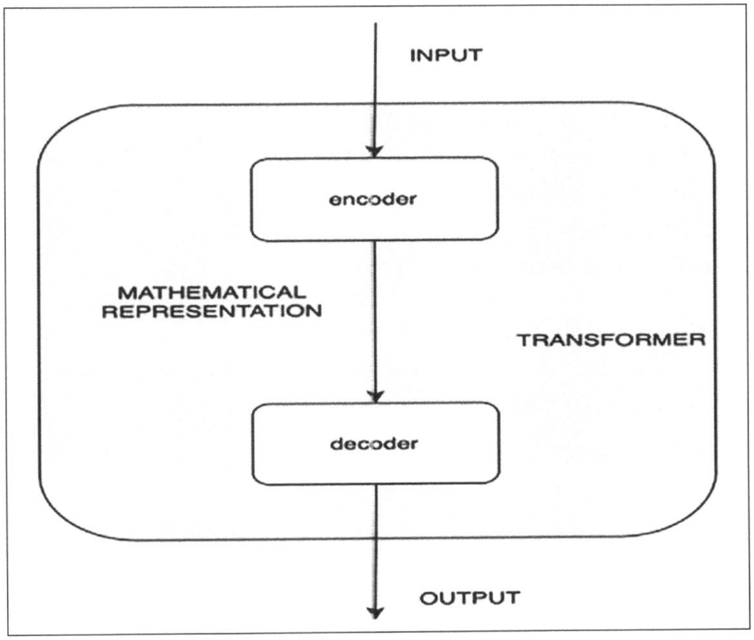

Figure 5.3: *Transformer Model*

At the heart of the transformer architecture lies the self-attention mechanism, which allows the model to weigh the importance of different input tokens based on their semantic relevance to each other. Unlike traditional recurrent neural networks (RNNs) or convolutional neural networks (CNNs), transformers process the entire input sequence in parallel, enabling efficient computation and effective modeling of long-range dependencies.

The key components of a transformer model include:

- **Multi-Head Self-Attention**: In this mechanism, the input sequence is transformed into query, key, and value vectors, which are then linearly projected into multiple heads. Each head independently computes attention scores, allowing the model to capture diverse aspects of the input sequence. The attention scores from different heads are concatenated and linearly transformed to produce the final attention output.
- **Positional Encoding**: Since transformers lack inherent sequential information such as RNNs, positional encoding is added to the input embeddings to convey the position of tokens within the sequence. This encoding, typically sinusoidal functions of different frequencies, enables the model to learn positional relationships between tokens and maintain sequential order.
- **Feedforward Neural Networks**: Following the self-attention layers, transformers include feedforward neural networks with a standard architecture consisting of fully connected layers and non-linear activation functions such as Rectified Linear Unit (ReLU). These networks provide additional capacity for modeling complex relationships within the data.
- **Layer Normalization and Residual Connections**: To stabilize training and facilitate the flow of gradients, transformers incorporate layer normalization and residual connections around each sub-layer, allowing for smoother optimization and deeper architectures without suffering from vanishing gradients.
- **Encoder-Decoder Architecture**: Transformers are commonly used in an encoder-decoder configuration for sequence-to-sequence tasks such as machine translation. The encoder processes the input sequence, while the decoder generates the output sequence autoregressively, attending to the encoder's output at each step.

The transformer architecture offers several advantages over traditional recurrent models:

- **Parallelization**: Transformers can process the entire input sequence in parallel, making them highly efficient for both training and inference, particularly on hardware accelerators such as GPUs and TPUs.
- **Long-Range Dependencies**: By leveraging self-attention mechanisms,

transformers excel at capturing long-range dependencies within sequences, enabling them to model intricate relationships and dependencies without suffering from the vanishing gradient problem.

- **Scalability**: Transformers are highly scalable and adaptable to sequences of varying lengths, making them suitable for a wide range of NLP tasks, from short text classification to long-form generation.

PyTorch provides comprehensive support for implementing transformer models, with libraries such as Hugging Face's Transformers offering pre-trained models and high-level APIs for fine-tuning and customization. By leveraging PyTorch's flexibility and efficiency, practitioners can harness the power of transformers to achieve state-of-the-art results in diverse NLP applications. In the subsequent sections, we delve into the implementation details of transformer models in PyTorch, exploring architectures such as BERT, GPT, and their variants, and demonstrating their effectiveness across different tasks and datasets.

Transfer Learning For NLP

Transfer learning has revolutionized the landscape of Natural Language Processing (NLP), enabling practitioners to leverage pre-trained language models and adapt them to downstream tasks with limited labeled data. This paradigm shift has significantly reduced the need for large, task-specific datasets and has democratized access to state-of-the-art NLP models, accelerating progress across various domains.

At the core of transfer learning for NLP lies the concept of pre-training and fine-tuning:

- **Pre-training**: Pre-training involves training a large language model on a vast corpus of text data using unsupervised learning objectives, such as language modeling or masked language modeling. During pre-training, the model learns to capture rich semantic representations of language, encoding knowledge about syntax, semantics, and world knowledge into its parameters. Notable examples of pre-trained language models include Bidirectional Encoder Representations from Transformers (BERT), Generative Pre-trained Transformer (GPT), and Robustly optimized BERT approach (RoBERTa).
- **Fine-tuning**: Fine-tuning refers to the process of adapting a pre-trained language model to a specific downstream task by further training it on task-specific labeled data. Instead of training the model from scratch, fine-tuning allows practitioners to transfer the knowledge encoded in the pre-trained model's parameters to the target task, thereby achieving competitive performance with significantly less data and computation. Fine-tuning typically involves updating a portion of the model's parameters while keeping the pre-trained weights fixed or applying differential learning rates to different layers of the model.

Transfer learning offers several advantages for NLP tasks:

- **Efficient Use of Data**: By leveraging pre-trained language models, transfer learning allows practitioners to utilize large-scale unlabeled text data for pre-training, thereby capturing rich linguistic patterns and semantic representations. Fine-tuning on task-specific datasets then enables the model to adapt to the nuances of the target task using a smaller amount of labeled data.
- **Generalization**: Pre-trained language models encode general linguistic knowledge learned from diverse text corpora, enabling them to generalize well across different tasks and domains. This generalization ability is particularly advantageous for tasks with limited labeled data or when the target task differs from the pre-training objectives.
- **Faster Iteration**: Transfer learning accelerates the development cycle for NLP applications by providing off-the-shelf pre-trained models that can be quickly adapted to new tasks or domains. This rapid iteration allows practitioners to experiment with different architectures, hyperparameters, and training strategies, facilitating faster innovation and prototyping.

Language Modeling with GPT-3.5

Language Modeling with GPT-3.5 represents a pinnacle in the evolution of Natural Language Processing (NLP), showcasing the capabilities of large-scale generative models trained on vast amounts of text data. GPT-3.5, an extension of the Generative Pre-trained Transformer (GPT) series developed by OpenAI, pushes the boundaries of language understanding and generation, demonstrating remarkable proficiency across a wide range of NLP tasks.

At its core, GPT-3.5 is a transformer-based language model trained on a diverse and extensive corpus of text data sourced from the internet. Unlike traditional task-specific models, GPT-3.5 is designed to exhibit strong generalization capabilities, enabling it to perform effectively across various NLP tasks without task-specific fine-tuning. This is achieved through its autoregressive generation approach, where the model generates text one token at a time based on its learned context.

Key features and characteristics of GPT-3.5 include:

- **Massive Scale**: GPT-3.5 is one of the largest language models ever created, consisting of billions of parameters. This immense scale allows it to capture intricate patterns and dependencies within language, facilitating more nuanced understanding and generation of text.
- **Zero-Shot and Few-Shot Learning**: One of the most notable capabilities of GPT-3.5 is its ability to perform zero-shot and few-shot learning, meaning it can generate coherent responses to prompts or tasks without explicit training

on those tasks. By providing a few examples or prompts, the model can adapt its behavior to perform specific tasks, such as text completion, question answering, or text summarization.

- **Versatility**: GPT-3.5 exhibits versatility in its application, capable of handling a wide range of NLP tasks, including text generation, translation, summarization, sentiment analysis, and more. Its ability to generalize across tasks without task-specific fine-tuning makes it particularly attractive for applications requiring flexibility and adaptability.
- **Contextual Understanding**: Through its transformer architecture and self-attention mechanisms, GPT-3.5 demonstrates strong contextual understanding of language. It can incorporate context from preceding tokens to generate coherent and contextually relevant responses, capturing nuances in meaning and tone.
- **Ethical and Safety Considerations**: Given its vast generative capabilities, GPT-3.5 raises important ethical and safety considerations regarding the potential misuse of AI-generated content, such as misinformation, biased outputs, or harmful content. Responsible deployment and monitoring of such models are essential to mitigate these risks and ensure their ethical use.

In practical terms, developers and researchers can interact with GPT-3.5 through APIs provided by OpenAI, enabling integration into various applications and platforms. The API allows users to input prompts or tasks and receive generated text outputs, leveraging the model's powerful generative capabilities in real-world scenarios.

Despite its impressive capabilities, GPT-3.5 is not without limitations. It may exhibit biases present in the training data, struggle with long-term coherence in generated text, and occasionally produce nonsensical or irrelevant responses. Understanding these limitations is crucial for responsible deployment and informed decision-making when utilizing GPT-3.5 in practical applications.

Conclusion

This chapter provided an in-depth exploration of cutting-edge methodologies and models that have reshaped the landscape of NLP. From Sequence-to-Sequence models to Attention Mechanisms, Transformer Models, Transfer Learning, and Language Modeling with GPT-3.5, we have traversed the frontier of NLP research and development, uncovering the intricacies of these advanced techniques and their practical applications.

Throughout this chapter, we have highlighted the versatility and power of PyTorch as a framework for implementing these state-of-the-art models. PyTorch's flexibility, efficiency, and extensive community support have enabled practitioners to experiment with complex architectures, fine-tune models for specific tasks, and achieve remarkable results across a wide range of NLP domains.

Furthermore, we have emphasized the importance of responsible AI deployment and ethical considerations, particularly in the context of large-scale language models such as GPT-3.5. As AI technologies continue to advance, it is crucial to prioritize ethical principles, fairness, and transparency in the development and deployment of NLP systems, ensuring they benefit society while minimizing potential risks and harms.

Looking ahead, the field of NLP is poised for further innovation and progress, driven by advances in deep learning, computational resources, and interdisciplinary collaboration. As practitioners continue to push the boundaries of what is possible with NLP, PyTorch will remain a foundational tool for researchers and developers, empowering them to explore new frontiers, tackle complex challenges, and unlock the full potential of natural language understanding and generation. In the next chapter, we will discuss model development, training, and evaluating NLP models using PyTorch.

Points to Remember

- **Sequence-to-Sequence Models**: Understand the encoder-decoder architecture and its applications in tasks such as machine translation and text summarization.
- **Attention Mechanisms**: Learn how attention mechanisms improve model performance by focusing on relevant parts of the input sequence during processing.
- **Transformer Models**: Explore the revolutionary transformer architecture, its self-attention mechanism, and its applications in various NLP tasks.
- **Transfer Learning for NLP**: Recognize the benefits of transfer learning in NLP, including efficient use of data, generalization across tasks, and faster iteration.
- **Language Modeling with GPT-3.5**: Appreciate the scale and versatility of GPT-3.5, its zero-shot and few-shot learning capabilities, and the ethical considerations surrounding its deployment.
- **PyTorch Integration**: Understand how PyTorch provides a flexible and efficient framework for implementing advanced NLP techniques, empowering practitioners to experiment with complex architectures and fine-tune models for specific tasks.
- **Ethical Considerations**: Be mindful of ethical implications when deploying advanced NLP models, such as biases in training data, potential misuse of AI-generated content, and the importance of responsible AI development and deployment.
- **Continuous Learning**: Stay updated with the latest advancements and research in the field of NLP, as the landscape continues to evolve rapidly with new methodologies, models, and applications.

Multiple Choice Questions

1. What is the primary function of attention mechanisms in NLP?
   a. To increase the computational efficiency of neural networks
   b. To enable models to focus on relevant parts of the input sequence
   c. To reduce the number of parameters in neural network architectures
   d. To prevent overfitting during model training
2. Which architecture introduced the revolutionary transformer model in NLP?
   a. Recurrent Neural Networks (RNNs)
   b. Convolutional Neural Networks (CNNs)
   c. Generative Pre-trained Transformer (GPT)
   d. Long Short-Term Memory (LSTM) networks
3. What advantage does transfer learning offer in NLP?
   a. It eliminates the need for labeled data in training NLP models
   b. It allows models to learn task-specific features from scratch
   c. It enables models to generalize across different tasks without fine-tuning
   d. It simplifies the training process by reducing the complexity of neural network architectures
4. What is a notable capability of GPT-3.5 in terms of learning?
   a. It requires extensive task-specific fine-tuning for optimal performance
   b. It can only generate text in languages for which it was explicitly trained
   c. It can perform zero-shot and few-shot learning without task-specific fine-tuning
   d. It relies solely on labeled data for generating text outputs
5. Which framework provides robust support for implementing advanced NLP techniques such as transformers and transfer learning?
   a. TensorFlow
   b. PyTorch
   c. Keras
   d. Scikit-learn

Answers

1. b
2. c
3. c
4. c
5. b

Questions

1. Describe the architecture of a Sequence-to-Sequence model and discuss its applications in NLP tasks.
2. How do attention mechanisms improve the performance of neural networks in natural language processing? Provide examples of tasks where attention mechanisms are particularly beneficial.
3. Explain the key components of a transformer model and discuss how it differs from traditional recurrent neural network (RNN) architectures in NLP.
4. What are the advantages of using transfer learning in NLP? How does transfer learning mitigate challenges associated with limited labeled data?
5. How does PyTorch facilitate the implementation of advanced NLP techniques, such as transformers and transfer learning? Provide examples of PyTorch functionalities that are particularly useful in NLP model development.
6. Reflect on the future directions of natural language processing research and development, considering the advancements discussed in this chapter. What challenges and opportunities lie ahead in the field of NLP, and how can practitioners contribute to its continued progress?

Key Terms

- **Sequence-to-Sequence Models**: Neural network architectures used for tasks where the input and output are both sequences of data. These models consist of an encoder that processes the input sequence and a decoder that generates the output sequence based on the encoder's representation.
- **Attention Mechanisms**: Components in neural network architectures that allow models to focus on specific parts of the input sequence during processing. Attention mechanisms enable better handling of long-range dependencies and improve the performance of sequence-based tasks.

- **Transformer Models**: A type of neural network architecture introduced in the paper "*Attention is All You Need*," which relies entirely on attention mechanisms and does not use recurrent connections. Transformers have become the standard for many NLP tasks due to their scalability and ability to capture long-range dependencies efficiently.
- **Transfer Learning**: A machine learning technique where knowledge gained from solving one task is applied to a different but related task. In NLP, transfer learning involves pre-training a language model on a large corpus of text data and then fine-tuning it on a specific downstream task with limited labeled data.
- **Language Modeling**: The task of predicting the probability distribution over the next word or token in a sequence given the previous words or tokens. Language models are trained to generate coherent and contextually relevant text.
- **GPT-3.5**: Generative Pre-trained Transformer 3.5, an advanced language model developed by OpenAI. GPT-3.5 is one of the largest language models ever created and is known for its zero-shot and few-shot learning capabilities, allowing it to perform a wide range of NLP tasks without task-specific fine-tuning.
- **PyTorch**: An open-source deep learning framework developed by Facebook's AI Research lab. PyTorch provides a flexible and efficient platform for implementing advanced NLP techniques, including transformers, attention mechanisms, and transfer learning.
- **Ethical Considerations**: Concerns and principles related to the responsible development and deployment of AI technologies, including NLP models. Ethical considerations in NLP may include issues such as bias in training data, fairness in model predictions, and the potential misuse of AI-generated content.

CHAPTER 6
Model Training and Evaluation

Introduction

In the field of Natural Language Processing (NLP), effective models rely not only on innovative architectures but also on robust training and evaluation methodologies. This chapter discusses model development, training, and evaluating NLP models using PyTorch.

We begin with dataset preparation, where the quality of data significantly defines the model's performance. Dataset preparation involves tasks of data acquisition, data preprocessing, and augmenting datasets to ensure they align with the specific NLP tasks.

In this chapter, we will also discuss the creation of a training dataset, as well as the evaluation of models once they are trained. Different evaluation metrics are considered for performing various NLP tasks such as classification, language generation, and sequence labeling.

Hyperparameter tuning follows, where we explore techniques to optimize model configurations for improved performance. This involves methods such as grid search, random search, and Bayesian optimization to navigate the vast parameter space effectively.

To overcome issues such as overfitting and ensure model generalization, we will discuss various regularization techniques such as dropout, L1/L2 regularization, and early stopping. These methods play a crucial role in preventing models from memorizing training data and enhancing their ability to generalize to unseen examples.

Structure

In this chapter, we will discuss the following topics:

- Dataset Preparation
- Training Pipelines
- Model Evaluation Metrics
- Hyperparameter Tuning
- Overfitting and Regularization Techniques

Dataset Preparation

Dataset preparation is a conducive initial step in building and training NLP models. The quality and suitability of the dataset directly impact the performance and generalization capabilities of the trained models. In this section, we explore the key considerations and techniques involved in dataset preparation for NLP tasks.

- **Data Sourcing**: This step involves the identification of relevant sources for acquiring data based on the specific NLP task (for example, text classification, named entity recognition, and machine translation).

  Data may be obtained through sources such as web scraping, public datasets (for example, Kaggle, UCI Machine Learning Repository), domain-specific corpora, or proprietary data.

- **Data Cleaning and Preprocessing**: Perform data cleaning to remove noise, irrelevant information, or duplicates. Preprocess raw text data through tokenization (splitting text into tokens or words), normalization (lowercasing, removing punctuation), and stemming/lemmatization to reduce variation and enhance consistency.

- **Data Augmentation**: Enhance dataset diversity and robustness by applying data augmentation techniques.

  Methods include synonym replacement, back translation, random insertion/deletion of words, or introducing typographical errors.

- **Splitting into Train, Validation, and Test Sets**: Divide the dataset into training, validation, and test sets for model training, tuning, and evaluation.

  We use a large portion for training (70%–80%), a smaller portion for validation (10%–15%), and a separate portion for final testing (10%–15%).

- **Resolve Imbalanced Data Issue**: Handle class imbalance issues by employing techniques such as oversampling minority classes, undersampling majority classes, or using class-weighted loss functions during training.

- **Utilizing PyTorch Data Utilities**: Leverage PyTorch's data handling utilities (for example, Dataset, DataLoader) for efficient data management and batch processing.

  Implement custom dataset classes to encapsulate data loading and preprocessing logic specific to the NLP task.

- **Exploratory Data Analysis (EDA)**: Conduct EDA to gain insights into the dataset's characteristics (for example, distribution of text lengths, class distribution).

Visualize data distributions and relationships to inform preprocessing and modeling decisions.

By meticulously preparing and preprocessing datasets using these techniques, practitioners lay a strong foundation for training robust and high-performing NLP models with PyTorch. The quality and diversity of the dataset significantly influence the model's ability to generalize and perform well on real-world tasks. Efficient dataset preparation is essential for achieving successful outcomes in NLP model development and deployment.

Training Pipelines

Training pipelines in the context of NLP refer to the systematic process of data preparation, training models, and evaluating performance. A well-organized training pipeline ensures efficient model development and optimization. This section will discuss the components required for designing effective training pipelines in PyTorch.

- **Data Loading and Batching**: We can use PyTorch's DataLoader to load and preprocess data efficiently.

  We can implement batch processing to feed batches of data into the model during training, reducing memory usage and improving training speed.

  ```
  from torch.utils.data import DataLoader
  train_loader = DataLoader(train_dataset, batch_size=32,
  shuffle=True)
  ```

- **Model Definition**: We can define the architecture of the NLP model using PyTorch's **`nn.Module`** and customize layers/modules based on the task (for example, RNNs, Transformers).

  We can incorporate embedding layers for text representation and define forward pass logic as follows:

  ```
  import torch.nn as nn
  class NLPModel(nn.Module):
      def __init__(self, vocab_size, embedding_dim, hidden_dim,
  num_classes):
  ```

```
        super(NLPModel, self).__init__()
        self.embedding = nn.Embedding(vocab_size, embedding_dim)
        self.rnn = nn.RNN(embedding_dim, hidden_dim, batch_
first=True)
        self.fc = nn.Linear(hidden_dim, num_classes)

    def forward(self, x):
        embedded = self.embedding(x)
        output, _ = self.rnn(embedded)
        logits = self.fc(output[:, -1, :])  # Get logits for the
last timestep
        return logits
```

- **Loss Function and Optimizer**: Define the loss function (for example, cross-entropy loss) suitable for the NLP task.

  Choose an optimizer (for example, Adam, SGD) to update model parameters based on computed gradients during training.

```
import torch.optim as optim
criterion = nn.CrossEntropyLoss()
optimizer = optim.Adam(model.parameters(), lr=0.001)
```

- **Training Loop**: Implement the training loop that iterates over batches of data, computes model predictions, calculates loss, and performs backpropagation to update model parameters.

```
num_epochs = 10
for epoch in range(num_epochs):
    model.train()
    for inputs, labels in train_loader:
        optimizer.zero_grad()
        outputs = model(inputs)
        loss = criterion(outputs, labels)
        loss.backward()
        optimizer.step()
```

- **Validation and Evaluation**: Periodically evaluate the model on a validation set to monitor performance and prevent overfitting.

  Compute evaluation metrics (for example, accuracy, F1-score) to assess model effectiveness.

- **Utilizing GPU Acceleration**: Utilize GPUs (if available) to accelerate model training using PyTorch's CUDA capabilities.

  Move the model and tensors to the GPU for faster computations.

```
device = torch.device('cuda' if torch.cuda.is_available() else
'cpu')
model.to(device)
```

- **Monitoring and Logging**: Use logging frameworks (for example, TensorBoard) to visualize training progress, monitor metrics, and track model performance across epochs.

By structuring training pipelines following these practices, developers can streamline model development, optimize training efficiency, and achieve superior performance in NLP tasks using PyTorch. Effective training pipelines are foundational for building scalable and robust NLP models.

Model Evaluation Metrics

Model evaluation metrics are essential for assessing the performance of Natural Language Processing (NLP) models trained using PyTorch. These metrics provide quantitative measures of how well the model performs on specific NLP tasks, such as text classification, named entity recognition, machine translation, sentiment analysis, and so on. Understanding and selecting appropriate evaluation metrics is crucial for interpreting model results and guiding further improvements. Here are some commonly used evaluation metrics in NLP:

- **Accuracy:**

  Definition: Accuracy measures the proportion of correct predictions (both true positives and true negatives) made by the model over all predictions.

  `Accuracy=(Number of Correct Predictions/Total Number of Predictions)×100%`

  In mathematical terms, this can be expressed as:

  `Accuracy=(TP+TN)/(TP+TN+FP+FN)×100%`

  Where:

  `TP` (True Positive) is the number of correctly predicted positive instances (for example, correctly predicted positive sentiment).

  `TN` (True Negative) is the number of correctly predicted negative instances (for example, correctly predicted negative sentiment).

  `FP` (False Positive) is the number of instances predicted as positive but are actually negative (Type I error).

  `FN` (False Negative) is the number of instances predicted as negative but are actually positive (Type II error).

  In this formula:

  1. `TP+TN` represents the total number of correct predictions.
  2. `TP+TN+FP+FN` represents the total number of predictions made by the model.

By multiplying the ratio of correct predictions to total predictions by 100%, we get the accuracy percentage, which indicates the proportion of correct predictions made by the model out of all predictions. A higher accuracy percentage indicates a more effective model in terms of making correct predictions across different classes or categories in a dataset.

- **Precision and Recall:**

  Precision:

  Precision measures the proportion of true positive predictions among all positive predictions made by the model.

  `Precision=True Positives/(True Positives + False Positives)`

  Recall:

  Recall measures the proportion of true positive predictions among all actual positive instances in the dataset.

  `Recall=True Positives/(True Positives + False Negatives)`

- **F1-score**:

  Definition: F1-score is the harmonic mean of precision and recall, providing a balanced measure that considers both false positives and false negatives.

  `Formula: F1=2×(Precision×Recall)/(Precision+Recall)`

- **Confusion Matrix:**

  Confusion Matrix is a table used to describe the performance of a classification model, showing the counts of true positives, true negatives, false positives, and false negatives.

  It provides insights into the types of errors made by the model, aiding in understanding its strengths and weaknesses.

  It provides a summary of the prediction results on a classification problem, especially for binary or multi-class problems. The confusion matrix helps in understanding the types of errors an algorithm is making and the distribution of those errors.

  A confusion matrix represents a two-dimensional table where:

  - Rows represent the actual classes (or true labels) of the data points.
  - Columns represent the predicted classes by the model.
    - In the case of binary classification, the confusion matrix is a 2×2 table.
    - For multi-class classification, the matrix grows in size (n × n), where n is the number of classes.

Structure of a Confusion Matrix (Binary Classification)

For binary classification, the confusion matrix has four key elements:

- **True Positives (TP):** The number of instances where the model correctly predicted the positive class (that is, both actual and predicted values are positive).
- **True Negatives (TN):** The number of instances where the model correctly predicted the negative class (that is, both actual and predicted values are negative).
- **False Positives (FP):** The number of instances where the model incorrectly predicted the positive class while the actual class was negative (also called a Type I Error).
- **False Negatives (FN):** The number of instances where the model incorrectly predicted the negative class, while the actual class was positive (also called a Type II Error).

Multi-Class Confusion Matrix

For multi-class classification, the confusion matrix expands to an n × n matrix, where n is the number of classes. Each element in this matrix represents the count of instances where the actual class is `i` and the predicted class is `j`.

- **Error Analysis**: By visualizing and analyzing a confusion matrix, one can see where the model is making mistakes (for example, if it confuses one class for another more often). This insight can help improve the model.

  Example: Confusion Matrix in Python

  ```
  from sklearn.metrics import confusion_matrix, classification_report
  from sklearn.model_selection import train_test_split
  from sklearn.datasets import load_iris
  from sklearn.ensemble import RandomForestClassifier # Load a sample
  dataset
  data = load_iris()
  X_train, X_test, y_train, y_test = train_test_split(data.data,
  data.target, test_size=0.3, random_state=42) # Train a classifier
  clf = RandomForestClassifier()
  clf.fit(X_train, y_train) # Make predictions
  y_pred = clf.predict(X_test) # Generate confusion matrix
  cm = confusion_matrix(y_test, y_pred) # Print confusion matrix
  and classification report print("Confusion Matrix:")
  print(cm) print("\nClassification Report:")
  print(classification_report(y_test, y_pred))
  ```

The output will show the confusion matrix and the classification report containing precision, recall, and f1-score for each class.

```
[[19  0  0]
 [ 0 13  0]
 [ 0  0 13]]

Classification Report:
              precision    recall  f1-score   support

           0       1.00      1.00      1.00        19
           1       1.00      1.00      1.00        13
           2       1.00      1.00      1.00        13

    accuracy                           1.00        45
   macro avg       1.00      1.00      1.00        45
weighted avg       1.00      1.00      1.00        45
```

***Figure 6.1**: Confusion matrix*

- **Limitations of the Confusion Matrix**
    - The matrix grows larger and more complex with increasing classes, making it harder to interpret visually.
    - Imbalance of Classes: Metrics such as accuracy derived from the confusion matrix can be misleading when the dataset is imbalanced. Alternative metrics such as F1-score or area under the ROC curve are often more informative.
    - The matrix is threshold-dependent, meaning the results can vary if the threshold used to classify probabilities is changed.
- **Bilingual Evaluation Understudy Score (BLEU Score):**

  Definition: Used for evaluating the quality of machine-translated text by comparing it to one or more reference translations.

  Use Case: Widely used in machine translation tasks to measure the overlap between predicted and reference translations.
- **Perplexity:**

  Definition: A measure of how well a probability distribution or language model predicts a sample, calculated as the exponentiation of the cross-entropy loss.

  It is usually used in language modeling tasks to assess the performance and fluency of generated text.

  Choosing the appropriate evaluation metric(s) depends on the specific NLP task and the desired balance between precision, recall, and other performance indicators. Evaluating models using multiple metrics provides a comprehensive understanding of their capabilities and limitations, guiding further iterations and improvements in model development. In PyTorch, these metrics can be computed and analyzed using libraries such as scikit-learn or custom implementations based on specific requirements.

Hyperparameter Tuning

Hyperparameter tuning is a crucial aspect of optimizing Natural Language Processing (NLP) models developed using PyTorch. Hyperparameters are parameters that are set before the learning process begins, unlike model parameters that are learned during training. Proper tuning of hyperparameters can significantly impact the performance and generalization of NLP models. In this section, we explore key concepts and techniques for hyperparameter tuning in PyTorch.

- **Types of Hyperparameters:**
  - **Learning Rate**: Controls the step size during gradient descent optimization. Too high a learning rate can lead to overshooting, while too low a learning rate can result in slow convergence.
  - **Batch Size**: Determines the number of samples processed in each iteration during training. A larger batch size can lead to faster convergence but may require more memory.
  - **Number of Epochs**: Specifies the number of times the entire dataset is passed through the model during training.
  - **Model Architecture Parameters**: Includes the number of layers, hidden units, dropout rates, and more.
- **Hyperparameter Tuning Techniques:**
  - **Grid Search**: Exhaustively searches a specified subset of hyperparameter values to find the combination that yields the best performance.
  - **Random Search**: Samples hyperparameter values randomly from a specified distribution, allowing for a more efficient search compared to grid search.
  - **Bayesian Optimization**: Uses probabilistic models to select hyperparameters based on past evaluations, aiming to find the optimal values more efficiently.
- **Cross-Validation:**
  - **K-Fold Cross-Validation**: Splits the dataset into K folds and iteratively uses K-1 folds for training and the remaining fold for validation. Helps in robustly evaluating hyperparameter performance and mitigating overfitting.

- **Hyperparameter Tuning Libraries:**
  - **Optuna**: A hyperparameter optimization framework that supports various optimization algorithms and integrates seamlessly with PyTorch.
  - **scikit-learn's `GridSearchCV` and `RandomizedSearchCV`**: Widely used libraries for grid search and random search hyperparameter tuning.
- **Monitoring and Visualization**:
  - **Learning Curves**: Plotting training/validation loss or other metrics against epochs to identify optimal hyperparameter values.
  - **Hyperparameter Importance**: Analyzing the impact of different hyperparameters on model performance using sensitivity analysis or feature importance techniques.

Start with a coarse search over a wide range of hyperparameters before refining the search around promising regions.

Use appropriate metrics (for example, validation loss, accuracy, F1-score) to evaluate model performance during hyperparameter tuning.

Consider the computational resources (for example, GPU availability, training time) when deciding the scope and granularity of the hyperparameter search.

By systematically tuning hyperparameters using these techniques, we can optimize the performance and efficiency of NLP models developed with PyTorch. Effective hyperparameter tuning plays a vital role in achieving state-of-the-art results and enhancing model robustness across different NLP tasks and datasets.

Overfitting and Regularization Techniques

Overfitting is a common challenge in machine learning, including Natural Language Processing (NLP), where a model learns to perform well on training data but fails to generalize to unseen data. Regularization techniques are employed to mitigate overfitting and improve the generalization ability of NLP models developed using PyTorch. In this section, we will explore the concept of overfitting and various regularization techniques that can be applied.

- **Understanding Overfitting:**

  Definition: Overfitting occurs when a model learns to capture noise and irrelevant patterns from the training data, resulting in poor performance on unseen data.

  Signs of Overfitting: Increasing training loss while validation loss remains stagnant or starts to increase; the model performs well on training data but poorly on validation/test data.

- **Regularization Techniques:**

  a. **L1 and L2 Regularization:**

  Purpose: Adds a penalty term to the loss function based on the L1 (sum of absolute values of weights) or L2 (sum of squared weights) norm of the model parameters.

  Effect: Encourages the model to learn simpler and smoother patterns, reducing the magnitude of parameter values and preventing overfitting.

  Implementation:

```
import torch.nn as nn
model = nn.Sequential(nn.Linear(20, 10), nn.ReLU(), nn.Linear(10,
1))# Apply L2 regularization to the optimizer
optimizer = torch.optim.SGD(model.parameters(), lr=0.01, weight_
decay=0.001)
```

  b. **Dropout**:

  Purpose: Randomly drops a proportion of units/neurons during training, preventing the model from relying too heavily on specific neurons and promoting ensemble-like behavior.

  Effect: Acts as a form of regularization by reducing interdependencies between neurons and enhancing model generalization.

  Implementation:

```
import torch.nn as nn
model = nn.Sequential(nn.Linear(20, 10), nn.ReLU(), nn.Dropout
(0.5), nn.Linear(10, 1))
```

  c. **Early Stopping:**

  Purpose: Halts the training process when the model's performance on a validation set stops improving.

  Effect: Prevents the model from overfitting to the training data by stopping training at the optimal point before performance degrades on unseen data.

  Implementation:

```
import numpy as np
from torch.utils.data import DataLoader
from sklearn.metrics import accuracy_score
# Example early stopping implementation
best_accuracy = 0.0
patience = 3
for epoch in range(num_epochs):
```

```
    # Training loop
    # Validation loop
    val_accuracy = compute_validation_accuracy(model, val_loader)
    if val_accuracy > best_accuracy:
        best_accuracy = val_accuracy
        # Save the best model checkpoint
        patience = 3
    else:
        patience -= 1
        if patience == 0:
            break
```

Practical Tips to Combat Overfitting

Use cross-validation to assess model performance across multiple data splits.

Monitor training and validation loss during model training and adjust regularization parameters accordingly.

Experiment with different regularization techniques and hyperparameters to find the optimal balance between bias and variance.

Applying appropriate regularization techniques in PyTorch-based NLP models is essential for improving model robustness, enhancing generalization capabilities, and achieving better performance on unseen data. By understanding the causes and consequences of overfitting and leveraging regularization effectively, practitioners can develop more reliable and effective NLP solutions.

Conclusion

In this chapter, we explored fundamental concepts and practical methodologies essential for developing and refining NLP models. Through careful dataset preparation, we learned the significance of sourcing and preprocessing data to ensure its suitability for specific tasks, setting the stage for effective model training.

The discussion then shifted towards the design of robust training pipelines within PyTorch, emphasizing efficient data loading, batching, and utilization of GPU resources to accelerate training. We underscored the importance of leveraging PyTorch's capabilities to streamline the training process and optimize model performance.

Moving to model evaluation, we explored a diverse range of evaluation metrics tailored to different NLP tasks, empowering readers to quantify model performance accurately. Additionally, we delved into hyperparameter tuning techniques, equipping practitioners with strategies to optimize model configurations for superior results.

A critical aspect covered in this chapter was the mitigation of overfitting through regularization techniques such as dropout and L1/L2 regularization, alongside methods such as early stopping. These strategies are pivotal for enhancing model generalization and robustness, ensuring their effectiveness beyond the training data.

Throughout our exploration, we highlighted practical implementation using PyTorch, providing code examples and best practices to facilitate hands-on learning. By integrating these methodologies into NLP projects, readers can leverage PyTorch's flexibility and efficiency to develop cutting-edge models capable of tackling real-world challenges.

As the NLP landscape continues to evolve, a solid foundation in model training and evaluation is indispensable. Armed with the insights gained from this chapter, readers are well-positioned to navigate the complexities of NLP model development, pushing the boundaries of what is achievable in natural language understanding and generation.

In the subsequent chapters, we will build upon this knowledge, exploring advanced techniques and applications that harness the full potential of PyTorch in NLP. Together, let us embark on a journey of discovery and innovation within the fascinating domain of NLP.

Points to Remember

- **Sequence-to-Sequence Models**: Understand the encoder-decoder architecture and its applications in tasks such as machine translation and text summarization.
- **Attention Mechanisms**: Learn how attention mechanisms improve model performance by focusing on relevant parts of the input sequence during processing.
- **Transformer Models**: Explore the revolutionary transformer architecture, its self-attention mechanism, and its applications in various NLP tasks.
- **Transfer Learning for NLP**: Recognize the benefits of transfer learning in NLP, including efficient use of data, generalization across tasks, and faster iteration.
- **Language Modeling with GPT-3.5**: Appreciate the scale and versatility of GPT-3.5, its zero-shot and few-shot learning capabilities, and the ethical considerations surrounding its deployment.
- **PyTorch Integration**: Understand how PyTorch provides a flexible and efficient framework for implementing advanced NLP techniques, empowering practitioners to experiment with complex architectures and fine-tune models for specific tasks.
- **Ethical Considerations**: Be mindful of ethical implications when deploying advanced NLP models, such as biases in training data, potential misuse of AI-generated content, and the importance of responsible AI development and deployment.

Multiple Choice Questions

1. What is a crucial step in dataset preparation for NLP tasks?
    a. Utilizing pre-trained models
    b. Randomly selecting data samples
    c. Sourcing and preprocessing data
    d. Performing hyperparameter tuning
2. Which PyTorch component is used for efficient data loading and batching during model training?
    a. DataLoader
    b. Transformer
    c. Optimizer
    d. Activation function
3. Which evaluation metric is commonly used for text classification tasks?
    a. BLEU score
    b. Precision-Recall curve
    c. F1-score
    d. Confusion matrix
4. What technique helps in optimizing model configurations by exploring different parameter values?
    a. Data augmentation
    b. Hyperparameter tuning
    c. Dropout regularization
    d. Gradient descent
5. Which method is effective for preventing overfitting during model training?
    a. Increasing the learning rate
    b. Adding more layers to the model
    c. Applying L1/L2 regularization
    d. Using a smaller batch size

Answers

1. c
2. a
3. c
4. b
5. c

Questions

1. Describe the importance of dataset preparation in NLP model development. What are some key considerations when sourcing and preprocessing data?
2. Explain the role of the DataLoader in PyTorch training pipelines. How does it facilitate efficient data loading and batching?
3. What are evaluation metrics, and why are they essential in assessing NLP model performance? Provide examples of evaluation metrics suitable for different NLP tasks.
4. Compare and contrast hyperparameter tuning techniques such as grid search, random search, and Bayesian optimization. When would you use each method in model development?
5. What is overfitting in the context of NLP models? How can regularization techniques such as dropout and L1/L2 regularization help mitigate overfitting?
6. Describe the steps involved in implementing dropout regularization in a PyTorch model. How does dropout prevent overfitting during training?
7. How does GPU acceleration benefit model training in PyTorch? Discuss the process of leveraging GPUs for faster computation during training.
8. Explain the concept of early stopping in model training. How does it prevent models from overfitting, and when should you apply this technique?
9. What are some practical strategies for optimizing training efficiency when working with large NLP datasets?
10. Discuss the importance of continuous learning and experimentation in NLP model development. How can practitioners stay updated with the latest advancements in PyTorch and NLP research?

Key Terms

- **DataLoader**: A utility in PyTorch used for efficient data loading and batching during model training. It enables parallel data loading, shuffling, and batching of samples, optimizing training performance.
- **Evaluation Metrics**: Quantitative measures used to assess the performance of NLP models on specific tasks. Examples include accuracy, precision, and recall, F1-score for classification tasks; BLEU score for machine translation; perplexity for language modeling; and so on.
- **Hyperparameter Tuning**: The process of optimizing model configurations (for example, learning rate, batch size, number of layers) to maximize performance. Techniques include grid search, random search, and Bayesian optimization.
- **Overfitting**: A phenomenon where a model learns to perform well on training data but fails to generalize to unseen data. Regularization techniques such as dropout, L1/L2 regularization. and early stopping are used to combat overfitting.
- **Regularization**: Techniques used to prevent overfitting and improve model generalization. Examples include dropout (randomly dropping units during training), L1/L2 regularization (adding penalties to the loss function based on the magnitude of model weights), and early stopping (halting training when validation performance stops improving).
- **GPU Acceleration**: Utilizing Graphics Processing Units (GPUs) to accelerate model training by parallelizing computations. PyTorch supports GPU acceleration, enabling faster training of deep learning models.
- **Early Stopping**: A regularization technique that involves monitoring model performance on a validation set during training and stopping the training process when performance starts to degrade, preventing overfitting.

CHAPTER 7
Improving NLP Models with PyTorch

Introduction

As we delve into the world of natural language processing (NLP), we find numerous challenges that may obstruct the performance and scalability of our NLP models. Overcoming these challenges is important for the development of robust, efficient, and interpretable NLP systems. This chapter, *Improving NLP Models with PyTorch*, discusses strategies and techniques that can enhance models, addressing several key areas that are pivotal for success in applied NLP.

One of the key issues in NLP is dealing with out-of-vocabulary (OOV) words. These are words that were not seen during a model's training phase and can severely impact the performance of NLP applications when they appear in new, unseen data. In this chapter, we will discuss the techniques, such as subword tokenization and character-level embeddings, that provide a way to handle OOV words by breaking down words into smaller, manageable units that are likely present in the training dataset.

This chapter discusses approaches such as truncated backpropagation through time and the use of hierarchical attention networks which help in dealing with issues related to long dependencies and large input sizes.

In this chapter, we will also cover how to use PyTorch's DataLoader class to streamline the process of creating and handling batches, ensuring that your model training is not only efficient but also scalable. This chapter also discusses techniques such as learning rate scheduling, gradient clipping, and the use of novel optimizer algorithms, namely AdamW, for improving the performance of NLP-based models. This chapter also discusses methods for interpreting and explaining model decisions, such as attention mechanisms and integrated gradients. These tools not only help in debugging and improving models but also ensure that end users can trust and rely on the automated decisions made by the models.

Structure

In this chapter, we will discuss the following topics:

- Handling Out-of-Vocabulary (OOV) Words
- Handling Long Sequences
- Batch Processing and Data Loaders
- Advanced Optimization Techniques
- Model Interpretability and Explainability

Handling Out-of-Vocabulary (OOV) Words

In natural language processing, out-of-vocabulary (OOV) words present a significant challenge. These are words that do not appear in the training dataset, and therefore, the model does not know how to handle them during inference or testing phases. Handling OOV words effectively is crucial for maintaining the performance and robustness of NLP models, especially in applications such as language translation, text summarization, and sentiment analysis, where new vocabulary can frequently appear.

OOV words can result from the following scenarios:

- **New Emerging Terms**: Language evolves rapidly with new slang, technical jargon, and neologisms.
- **Domain-Specific Vocabulary**: Words specific to certain fields or interests may not appear in a general training corpus.
- **Misspellings and Variations**: Different spellings or morphological variations of words can also be treated as OOV.

Strategies for Handling OOV Words include the following:

- **Subword Tokenization:**
    - **Byte Pair Encoding (BPE)**: BPE iteratively merges the most frequent pair of bytes or characters in a given text data, which helps in splitting words into the most frequent subwords. This approach is particularly useful for handling infrequent words and is widely used in models such as Generative Pre-trained Transformer (GPT) and Bidirectional Encoder Representations from Transformers (BERT).
    - **WordPiece**: Similar to BPE, WordPiece models the vocabulary as a set of subword units, which are used to break down unknown words into known subwords.

 - **SentencePiece**: This model treats the input as a raw stream and learns to segment it into a suitable subword vocabulary, handling space as just another character that can be encoded, thus simplifying preprocessing.

- **Character-Level Embeddings:**

  Instead of using word-level embeddings, character-level embeddings process words at the character level. This allows the model to understand and generate embeddings for any word, regardless of whether it has seen it before, by learning the representations based on character combinations.

- **Out-of-Vocabulary Bucket:**

  A common and straightforward approach is to assign all OOV words to a special token such as `<UNK>` (unknown). This technique, while simple, often results in a loss of information and can degrade the performance if the number of OOV words is large.

- **Morphological Decomposition:**

  Decomposing words into morphemes, the smallest meaningful units of language, can help in handling words unseen during training. This is particularly useful for agglutinative languages such as Turkish, where many words can be formed by combining morphemes.

- **Synthetic Data Generation:**

  Generating synthetic data by introducing artificial OOV words during training can help the model learn to cope with new words during inference.

- **Zero-Shot Learning and Transfer Learning:**

  Leveraging models trained on massive datasets can reduce the impact of OOV words, as these models are likely to have encountered a broader vocabulary. Techniques such as transfer learning, where a pre-trained model is fine-tuned on a specific task, can also help mitigate the OOV problem.

Handling OOV words is a critical aspect of developing robust NLP systems. By employing strategies such as subword tokenization, character-level embeddings, and synthetic data generation, developers can enhance model generalization and ensure that NLP applications remain effective and accurate even in the face of unfamiliar words. These strategies not only improve the handling of OOV words but also contribute to the overall adaptability and flexibility of NLP models in real-world applications.

Handling Long Sequences

Long sequences of text pose significant challenges in natural language processing (NLP), particularly for tasks such as text summarization, machine translation, and document classification.

The challenges of Long Sequences include the following:

- **Memory Constraints**: Recurrent Neural Networks (RNNs), including their more advanced variants such as Long Short-Term Memory (LSTM) networks and Gated Recurrent Units (GRUs), can struggle with memory usage when processing lengthy sequences.
- **Vanishing and Exploding Gradients**: These issues are prevalent in sequence models due to the compounding effects of gradients during backpropagation over many time steps.
- **Computational Efficiency**: Processing long sequences can be computationally expensive and time-consuming, especially when the dependencies between the elements are complex.
- **Loss of Information**: Traditional models might lose information from the initial segments of the text as more data is processed, particularly in simple RNNs.

Strategies for Handling Long Sequences include the following:

- **Truncated Backpropagation Through Time (TBPTT):** This technique involves backpropagating errors only for a limited number of steps instead of over the entire length of the sequence. TBPTT reduces the computational burden and helps manage the vanishing gradient problem by limiting the sequence length during each training pass.
- **Attention Mechanisms**: Attention models allow the network to focus on different parts of the input sequence for each step of the output sequence, effectively creating shortcuts between long-range dependencies. This method is particularly effective in tasks such as translation, where each output word may be influenced more by specific parts of the input rather than by its immediate neighbors.

  Transformers, which rely solely on attention mechanisms and dispense with recurrence entirely, are particularly adept at managing long sequences. They parallelize better and are more scalable compared to RNN-based approaches.
- **Hierarchical Attention Networks**: These networks structure the data processing hierarchically (for example, words to sentences to documents) and apply attention mechanisms at each level, reducing the complexity of handling very long texts by breaking them into manageable chunks.
- **Sequence Bucketing**: Grouping sequences of similar lengths into the same batch can reduce the number of padding tokens required, which decreases memory usage and improves processing time.
- **Stateful RNNs**: In stateful RNNs, the final hidden states of one batch are used as the initial hidden states for the next batch, allowing the model to maintain state across many sequences. This can be particularly useful when sequences

are too long to process in a single batch but can be segmented across multiple batches.

- **Gradient Clipping**: This technique limits the size of gradients to a defined maximum to prevent exploding gradients, which can be a severe problem in training over long sequences.

By effectively implementing the aforementioned strategies, NLP models can become more robust, efficient, and capable of capturing the complexities inherent in lengthy textual data, thereby improving both performance and practical applicability in real-world scenarios.

Batch Processing and Data Loaders

Batch processing is a fundamental aspect of training neural networks in NLP. It involves processing data in batches, rather than individually or all at once, which can significantly improve computational efficiency, make better use of hardware resources, and stabilize the training process. Data loaders are utilities or components designed to automate the process of loading, transforming, and batching data, thereby facilitating a smooth training pipeline.

Advantages of Batch Processing in the context of machine learning and NLP are:

- **Efficiency**: Processing data in batches allows for computational optimizations such as parallel processing. This makes better use of the underlying hardware, such as GPUs, which are designed to perform operations on multiple data points simultaneously.
- **Generalization**: Training with batches helps to minimize the noise in the gradient updates. Each batch provides a more general representation of the dataset, reducing the variance in updates compared to single data point (stochastic) training.
- **Stability**: Larger batches result in smoother learning curves as the updates become less susceptible to outliers and noise in the data.

While batch processing is beneficial, it comes with challenges:

- **Memory Constraints**: The size of batches is often limited by the amount of memory available, especially on GPUs.
- **Optimal Batch Size**: Finding the optimal batch size can be a trade-off between training speed and model performance. Too large a batch can lead to poor generalization, while too small a batch may result in unstable training dynamics.
- **Non-Uniform Sequence Lengths**: NLP data often consists of sequences of varying lengths, which complicates batch processing because each batch needs to have tensors of the same shape.

Data Loaders in PyTorch

PyTorch provides an efficient framework for data loading with its **`torch.utils.data.DataLoader`** class, which can be used to handle the complexities:

- **Automatic Batching**: The DataLoader automatically collates individual data points into batches using a collate function, which can be customized to handle the specific requirements of the dataset, such as padding sequences to a common length within a batch.
- **Shuffling**: It supports random shuffling of data, which is crucial for training neural networks effectively, preventing the model from learning the order of the data.
- **Parallel Data Loading**: DataLoader supports parallel data processing using multiple worker threads, which helps in loading data asynchronously and speeding up training.

Implementing Effective Data Loaders

Here are some considerations for implementing effective data loaders in NLP:

- **Padding and Dynamic Batching**: To handle sequences of varying lengths, implement dynamic padding where each batch pads its sequences to the length of the longest sequence in that batch. Alternatively, dynamic batching can be used where sequences of similar lengths are grouped together to minimize padding.
- **Custom Collate Functions**: Customize the collate function used by the DataLoader to handle specific preprocessing steps such as tokenization, numericalization, and padding.
- **Resource Management**: Efficiently manage resources by choosing an appropriate number of worker threads in the DataLoader to balance between data loading speed and CPU usage.

Batch processing and data loaders are pivotal in building efficient and effective NLP models. They streamline the training process and optimize resource utilization, which is essential for handling large datasets in NLP.

Advanced Optimization Techniques

Optimization is a critical component of training neural networks, including those used in natural language processing (NLP). While basic techniques such as stochastic gradient descent (SGD) are widely used, advanced optimization algorithms can significantly improve the training speed, convergence rate, and overall performance of NLP models.

In NLP, the models often deal with high-dimensional data and complex model architectures. Challenges such as vanishing and exploding gradients, slow convergence, and getting stuck in local minima are common. Efficiently overcoming these challenges necessitates the use of advanced optimization techniques.

Advanced Optimization Algorithms

In this section, we will discuss advanced optimization algorithms. These are:

- **Adaptive Moment Estimation (Adam)**

  Adam combines the advantages of two other extensions of stochastic gradient descent. Specifically:

  - Adaptive Gradient Algorithm (AdaGrad) that maintains a per-parameter learning rate that improves performance on problems with sparse gradients (such as word embeddings).
  - Root Mean Square Propagation (RMSProp) that also maintains per-parameter learning rates that are adapted based on the average of recent magnitudes of the gradients for the weight (which works well in online and non-stationary settings).

  Adam is computationally efficient, has little memory requirements, is invariant to diagonal rescale of the gradients, and is well suited for problems that are large in terms of data and/or parameters.

  Adam also automatically tunes itself and generally requires less configuration in terms of learning rate settings.

- **Adam with Weight Decay (AdamW)**

  AdamW modifies the standard Adam optimizer to handle weight decay separately from other hyperparameters, resulting in better training convergence.

  This optimizer separates the weight decay from the optimization steps taken with respect to. the loss function. It corrects the problem with Adam's application of L2 regularization and often results in better training outcomes.

- **Nesterov Accelerated Gradient (NAG)**

  NAG is a variant of momentum SGD that provides a more responsive approach to course corrections. It anticipates the future position of parameters based on current momentum, effectively looking ahead by correcting the gradient of the update step.

  This anticipation allows NAG to perform better than standard momentum and often results in faster convergence.

- **BFGS and Limited-memory BFGS (L-BFGS)**

  BFGS and L-BFGS are more sophisticated quasi-Newton methods that use a set of past gradients to estimate the inverse Hessian matrix of the second derivatives. This approach provides a more accurate direction for the next step.

  L-BFGS is particularly well suited for NLP tasks involving a large number of parameters and where memory constraints prevent the full BFGS method from being used. It has been shown to be effective in training deep neural networks with large-scale data.

- **Gradient Clipping**

  Gradient clipping is a technique used to tackle the exploding gradients problem. It involves clipping the gradients of a model during training to a defined range or norm value, which ensures that the gradients do not become too large, which can destabilize the training process.

  It is widely used in training recurrent neural networks, where long sequences can result in very large updates.

Implementing Optimization Techniques in PyTorch

In PyTorch, these optimizers are readily available and can be easily integrated into the training loop. Here is a basic example of using the Adam optimizer:

```
import torch.optim as optim
# Assuming `model` is your neural network and `data_loader` is
your data-loading pipeline
optimizer = optim.Adam(model.parameters(), lr=0.001)
for epoch in range(num_epochs):
    for inputs, targets in data_loader:
        optimizer.zero_grad()
        outputs = model(inputs)
        loss = loss_function(outputs, targets)
        loss.backward()
        optimizer.step()
```

Model Interpretability and Explainability

As natural language processing (NLP) models become more complex and widely used in critical applications, the need for interpretability and explainability of these models has grown abundantly. Interpretability refers to the extent to which a human can understand the cause of a decision made by a model, while explainability involves the ability to explain, in human terms, the mechanisms behind model predictions. This section delves into why these concepts are essential in NLP and explores techniques and methodologies to achieve them.

Importance of Interpretability and Explainability

Following are the terms pertaining to Interpretability and Explainability:

- **Trust**: Users are more likely to trust a model if its decisions can be understood and justified.
- **Debugging**: Understanding how a model makes decisions can help developers identify and correct errors.
- **Regulatory Compliance**: In many industries, regulations may require explanations of decisions made by automated systems.
- **Model Improvement**: Insights from model predictions can provide valuable feedback into the modeling process, helping to refine and improve models.

Techniques for Improving Interpretability and Explainability

Here are the techniques to improve Interpretability and Explainability:

- **Feature Importance:** Techniques such as permutation importance and SHapley Additive exPlanations (SHAP) values can be used to determine which features are most influential in a model's predictions. This is particularly useful in models where input features are easily interpretable (for example, tabular data).
- **Attention Mechanisms:** The Attention Mechanism is a crucial concept in modern machine learning, particularly in Natural Language Processing (NLP) and computer vision.

  It allows models to focus on specific parts of the input data, giving more importance (or "*attention*") to certain parts that are more relevant to the task at hand.

  In simpler models, namely Recurrent Neural Networks (RNNs), the entire input sequence is passed through the model, and each input element is treated with equal importance. This can be a problem for longer sequences because earlier inputs can get "*forgotten*" as the model processes more data. The Attention Mechanism addresses this by allowing the model to focus on specific parts of the input sequence at each step, enabling it to capture long-range dependencies and improving performance in tasks such as translation, summarization, and image captioning.

Working of Attention Mechanism

In an encoder-decoder model:

- **Encoder**: Converts the input sequence (for example, a sentence) into a set of hidden states, one for each time step.
- **Attention**: At each time step, the attention mechanism computes a score for each hidden state based on how important it is to the current time step in the decoder. The score is typically computed using a similarity function (such as a dot product or a feedforward neural network).
- **Weights**: These scores are converted into attention weights using a `softmax` function, which ensures that the weights sum to 1. Each weight represents how much focus should be placed on a specific part of the input sequence.
- **Context Vector**: The attention weights are used to compute a weighted sum of the encoder's hidden states, resulting in a context vector.
- **Decoder**: The context vector is used by the decoder to generate the next output in the sequence. This process is repeated for each time step in the decoder.

Types of Attention Mechanisms:

- **Additive Attention (Bahdanau Attention)**: Uses a feedforward neural network to compute the similarity between the current decoder hidden state and the encoder hidden states.
- **Dot-Product Attention (Luong Attention)**: Uses the dot product between the current decoder hidden state and each encoder hidden state to compute similarity.
- **Self-Attention**: Each element of the input sequence attends to every other element of the sequence. This is widely used in the Transformer model, which does not require RNNs at all and uses only attention mechanisms for sequence modeling.

PyTorch Implementation of Attention Mechanism

```
import torch
import torch.nn as nn
import torch.nn.functional as F
class Attention(nn.Module):
def __init__(self, hidden_size):
super(Attention, self).__init__() # Linear layer to calculate attention
scores       self.attention = nn.Linear(hidden_size, hidden_size)
def forward(self, encoder_outputs, hidden_state):
hidden_state_expanded=hidden_state.unsqueeze(1).expand_as(encoder_outputs)
attention_scores = torch.tanh(self.attention(encoder_outputs))
```

```
scores = torch.sum(attention_scores * hidden_state_expanded, dim=2)
attention_weights = F.softmax(scores, dim=1)
context_vector = torch.bmm(attention_weights.unsqueeze(1), encoder_
outputs)
 return context_vector, attention_weights
encoder_outputs = torch.rand(batch_size, seq_len, hidden_size)
hidden_state = torch.rand(batch_size, hidden_size)
attention_layer = Attention(hidden_size)
attention_weights = attention_layer(encoder_outputs, hidden_state)
print("Context Vector:", context_vector.shape)
print("Attention Weights:", attention_weights.shape)
```

In the preceding code, we define an `**Attention**` class that takes in the **encoder_outputs** (all the hidden states of the encoder) and a **hidden_state** (the decoder hidden state at the current time step). The attention scores (**attention_weights**) are calculated by applying a linear transformation followed by a dot product between the encoder outputs and the hidden state. Then we use the **softmax** function to normalize the scores into attention weights. The context vector is computed by multiplying the attention weights by the encoder outputs, resulting in a weighted sum of the encoder hidden states. The resulting `**context_vector**` is then passed to the decoder, which uses it to generate the next word in the output sequence.

Local Interpretable Model-agnostic Explanations (LIME)

LIME is a technique that approximates a complex model locally with a simpler one that is easier to understand. By perturbing the input data and observing the changes in outputs, LIME identifies which features significantly influence the output. It is a technique designed to explain the predictions of any machine learning model in an interpretable and intuitive way. It aims to answer the question: Why did a particular model make a certain prediction? In modern machine learning, many models, such as deep neural networks, ensemble methods (for example, random forests or gradient boosting), and support vector machines, are often referred to as "*black boxes*" because their internal decision-making processes are complex and difficult to interpret. LIME helps explain these models by providing locally interpretable explanations for individual predictions.

Key Concepts in LIME:

- **Model Agnostic**: LIME can explain any model (classification, regression, neural networks, tree-based models, and so on). It treats the machine learning model as a black box and does not require access to the internal structure or parameters of the model.
- **Local Explanations**: Instead of trying to explain the global behavior of the model (which is often too complex), LIME focuses on explaining individual

predictions by approximating the model locally around the specific data point of interest. This is based on the idea that the model's behavior is often more interpretable in a small neighborhood of the data.

- **Interpretable Model**: LIME builds an interpretable model, such as a linear model, decision tree, or a simpler approximation, to explain the prediction for a particular instance.

The process of LIME involves the following steps:

1. **Select the Instance to Explain**: Suppose you have a black-box model that makes predictions, and you want to understand why the model made a certain prediction for a particular instance (for example, a certain image or text).

2. **Generate Perturbations (Synthetic Data Points)**: LIME generates synthetic data points around the instance by perturbing the input. For example, if the input is an image, it may modify the image by turning off certain parts (for instance, superpixels). If it is a text, LIME might modify words or replace them with other words. These perturbations allow LIME to see how the model reacts to small changes in the input.

3. **Get Model Predictions for Perturbations**: For each of these perturbed instances, LIME queries the black-box model and gets the model's predictions. This provides insight into how the model behaves locally around the instance of interest.

4. **Fit an Interpretable Model**: LIME then fits an interpretable model (such as a linear regression or decision tree) to explain the black-box model's behavior in this local region. This simple model uses the synthetic data points as features and their corresponding predictions from the black-box model as the target values.

5. **Explain the Prediction**: The simple, interpretable model is used to provide an explanation for why the black-box model made a particular prediction for the original instance. The explanation often takes the form of feature importance or how much each feature contributed to the prediction.

6. **Example of LIME**: Suppose we have a machine learning model that predicts whether a person will default on a loan. The model takes several inputs, such as income, age, loan amount, credit score, and more. Now, LIME could explain why the model predicted '*default*' for a particular individual by focusing on that instance and fitting a simpler model that shows the contribution of each feature (for example, credit score, income) to the '*default*' prediction.

LIME for Different Data Types:

- **Tabular Data (Structured Data):** LIME can explain predictions for models that work on structured/tabular data (such as classification models for loan defaults, fraud detection, and so on). It examines how changes in specific features (for example, income, loan amount) impact the model's prediction.

- **Text Data**: For NLP tasks, LIME perturbs the text by removing or replacing words and then observes how those changes impact the prediction. For instance, in a sentiment analysis model, LIME can show which words contributed most to a "*positive*" or "*negative*" prediction.
- **Image Data**: LIME can explain image classification models by breaking down an image into superpixels (small, contiguous regions) and observing how the prediction changes when parts of the image are masked or altered. This helps identify which parts of the image contributed most to a particular prediction.

Strengths of LIME:

- **Model Agnostic**: LIME works with any machine learning model, making it versatile across different applications.
- **Local Interpretability**: LIME focuses on local behavior, which makes it easier to understand individual predictions rather than explaining the entire model globally.
- **Flexibility**: LIME can be applied to a wide range of data types (text, tabular, images), allowing it to be used across diverse applications.

Limitations of LIME :

- **Approximation Quality**: The explanation provided by LIME is based on a local approximation, which may not always accurately reflect the true decision-making process of the black-box model, especially if the model behaves erratically in certain regions.
- **Computational Cost**: Generating perturbed instances and querying the black-box model for each of them can be computationally expensive, particularly for large datasets or models with slow inference times.
- **Perturbation Strategy**: The way LIME perturbs the data can affect the quality of the explanation. Poor perturbation strategies may result in misleading interpretations.
- **Interpretability of the Explanation**: While the explanations generated by LIME are simpler than the original model, they may still not be intuitive for non-expert users, especially in high-dimensional datasets.

Example of Python in LIME:

```
!pip install lime
import numpy as np
import sklearn
import sklearn.datasets
import sklearn.ensemble
```

```
from lime import lime_tabular
# Load a dataset (Breast Cancer dataset for classification)
data = sklearn.datasets.load_breast_cancer()
X = data['data'] y = data['target']
# Split into train and test datasets
from sklearn.model_selection import train_test_split
X_train, X_test, y_train, y_test = train_test_split(X, y, test_size=0.2,
random_state=42) # Train a random forest classifier
rf = sklearn.ensemble.RandomForestClassifier(n_estimators=100)
rf.fit(X_train, y_train) # Initialize LIME explainer for tabular data
explainer = lime_tabular.LimeTabularExplainer(X_train, feature_names=-
data['feature_names'], class_names=['malignant', 'benign'], discretize_
continuous=True)
# Select an instance to explain (for example, the first test instance)
 i = 0
instance = X_test[i] # Generate explanation for the selected instance
exp = explainer.explain_instance(instance, rf.predict_proba, num_fea-
tures=5)
# Print the explanation (weights of the top features)
exp.show_in_notebook()
```

In the preceding code, **`LimeTabularExplainer`** initializes the LIME explainer for structured/tabular data. **`explain_instance`** generates an explanation for a specific instance of interest by approximating the behavior of the random forest classifier around that instance. The output is a set of feature importance showing which features contributed most to the model's prediction.

- **Layer-wise Relevance Propagation (LRP):** LRP backpropagates the output prediction of a neural network back to the input layer to determine the relevance of each input feature in producing a particular output. This is especially helpful in deep learning models where direct feature importance is not straightforward.
- **Visualization Tools:** Tools such as t-SNE and PCA for dimensionality reduction can be used to visualize high-dimensional data and embeddings. Visualizing the activation of different layers in a network can also help understand what features the model is focusing on.

For sequence tasks, visualizing attention weights across inputs can show how different parts of the input sequence affect the outputs.

Challenges in NLP Model Interpretability:

- **Complexity of Models**: Deep learning models, particularly those used in NLP, are often considered "*black boxes*" because of their complexity and the high number of parameters.
- **Subjectivity of Language**: Language is inherently subjective and context-dependent, which can make consistent interpretations challenging.

- **Scalability of Techniques**: Some interpretability techniques are computationally intensive or not scalable to very large models or datasets.

Conclusion

In this chapter, we explored a variety of advanced techniques aimed at overcoming common challenges in natural language processing using PyTorch. From handling out-of-vocabulary words to optimizing the processing of long sequences, the strategies presented here are designed to refine and enhance the performance of the NLP models.

We discussed dealing with the problem of out-of-vocabulary words, introducing you to innovative techniques such as subword tokenization and character-level embeddings, which are crucial for enhancing model robustness in the case of unfamiliar inputs. We also discussed dealing with long sequences, where we learned about methods such as truncated backpropagation and hierarchical attention networks to effectively handle long dependencies and improve memory utilization.

This chapter also discussed the critical role of batch processing and the efficient use of PyTorch's DataLoader to streamline the workflows and improve computational efficiency. It delved into the increasingly important area of model interpretability and explainability. By integrating tools such as attention mechanisms and integrated gradients, it not only boosts the transparency of NLP models but also increases the trust and reliability of their decisions in real-world applications.

The strategies covered in this chapter are not just solutions to current challenges but are also stepping stones to future innovations in natural language processing. The insights from this chapter will help you build more robust, efficient, and interpretable NLP systems using PyTorch. In the next chapter, we will explore the transition of NLP models from research experiments to practical solutions.

Points to Remember

- Utilize subword tokenization and character-level embeddings to manage OOV words effectively.
- Address memory constraints and capture long-range dependencies by employing strategies such as truncated backpropagation through time and hierarchical attention networks.
- Sequence segmentation and stateful RNNs may be used to maintain context over long texts without overwhelming the model.
- For data handling and to enable batch processing, use PyTorch's DataLoader which is crucial for training models on large datasets.
- Implement and prioritize methods that enhance the transparency of the model, such as attention mechanisms and tools such as LIME or SHAP for feature importance.

- Interpretability is not just for user trust but also for debugging and improving model performance by understanding its decision-making process.
- Early detection of problems with model generalization can be facilitated by routine testing and validation on a variety of data sets.

Multiple Choice Questions

1. What is the primary reason for using subword tokenization in NLP models?
   a. To increase the model's speed
   b. To handle out-of-vocabulary words
   c. To reduce the size of the model
   d. To improve the model's accuracy on seen words
2. Which technique is beneficial for managing long sequences in NLP?
   a. Batch normalization
   b. Truncated backpropagation through time
   c. Dropout
   d. Max pooling
3. What does PyTorch's DataLoader primarily help with?
   a. Optimizing the model's parameters
   b. Managing GPU memory usage
   c. Creating and managing batches of data
   d. Visualizing data distributions
4. Which optimizer is known for combining the advantages of two other optimizers while adding a correction term for the first moment?
   a. SGD
   b. RMSprop
   c. Adam
   d. Adagrad
5. Gradient clipping is used in training neural networks to:
   a. Increase the gradient flow
   b. Prevent the vanishing gradient problem

   c. Prevent the exploding gradient problem
   d. Reduce computational complexity
6. What aspect of model training does learning rate scheduling directly affect?
   a. Model size
   b. Convergence speed
   c. Batch size
   d. Feature selection
7. Which method can be used to increase the interpretability of an NLP model?
   a. L1 regularization
   b. Attention mechanisms
   c. Data augmentation
   d. Cross-validation
8. Hierarchical attention networks are particularly useful for:
   a. Reducing the computational cost
   b. Speeding up the inference
   c. Simplifying model architecture
   d. Handling long sequences
9. What is the primary use of character-level embeddings?
   a. To handle out-of-vocabulary words
   b. To improve translation accuracy
   c. To reduce model training time
   d. To increase batch processing speed
10. Integrated gradients are used for:
    a. Optimizing batch size
    b. Adjusting learning rates
    c. Understanding model predictions
    d. Balancing class distribution

11. AdamW differs from Adam by:
    a. Not using momentum
    b. Using a different learning rate
    c. Modifying the weight decay approach
    d. Eliminating the bias correction
12. In the context of NLP, truncated backpropagation through time is used to:
    a. Shorten the total training time
    b. Process data in smaller, manageable batches
    c. Reduce the computational complexity in processing sequences
    d. Prevent data leakage
13. Which of the following is not typically addressed by model explainability techniques?
    a. How model weights are initialized
    b. Why specific predictions are made
    c. Which features influence model decisions
    d. How to improve model transparency
14. What is a major challenge when handling long sequences in NLP models?
    a. Capturing long-range dependencies
    b. Increasing the number of parameters
    c. Decreasing model accuracy
    d. Simplifying model architectures

Answers

1. b
2. b
3. c
4. c
5. c

6. b
7. b
8. d
9. a
10. c
11. c
12. c
13. a
14. a

Questions

1. Describe the importance of dataset preparation in NLP model development. What are some key considerations when sourcing and preprocessing data?
2. Explain the role of the DataLoader in PyTorch training pipelines. How does it facilitate efficient data loading and batching?
3. What are evaluation metrics, and why are they essential in assessing NLP model performance? Provide examples of evaluation metrics suitable for different NLP tasks.
4. Compare and contrast hyperparameter tuning techniques such as grid search, random search, and Bayesian optimization. When would you use each method in model development?
5. What is overfitting in the context of NLP models? How can regularization techniques such as dropout and L1/L2 regularization help mitigate overfitting?
6. Describe the steps involved in implementing dropout regularization in a PyTorch model. How does dropout prevent overfitting during training?
7. How does GPU acceleration benefit model training in PyTorch? Discuss the process of leveraging GPUs for faster computation during training.
8. Explain the concept of early stopping in model training. How does it prevent models from overfitting, and when should you apply this technique?
9. What are some practical strategies for optimizing training efficiency when working with large NLP datasets?

10. Discuss the importance of continuous learning and experimentation in NLP model development. How can practitioners stay updated with the latest advancements in PyTorch and NLP research?

Key Terms

- **DataLoader**: A utility in PyTorch used for efficient data loading and batching during model training. It enables parallel data loading, shuffling, and batching of samples, optimizing training performance.
- **Evaluation Metrics**: Quantitative measures used to assess the performance of NLP models on specific tasks. Examples include accuracy, precision, recall, and F1-score for classification tasks; BLEU score for machine translation; perplexity for language modeling; and more.
- **Hyperparameter Tuning**: The process of optimizing model configurations (for example, learning rate, batch size, number of layers) to maximize performance. Techniques include grid search, random search, and Bayesian optimization.
- **Overfitting**: A phenomenon where a model learns to perform well on training data but fails to generalize to unseen data. Regularization techniques such as dropout, L1/L2 regularization, and early stopping are used to combat overfitting.
- **Regularization**: Techniques used to prevent overfitting and improve model generalization. Examples include dropout (randomly dropping units during training), L1/L2 regularization (adding penalties to the loss function based on the magnitude of model weights), and early stopping (halting training when validation performance stops improving).
- **GPU Acceleration**: Utilizing Graphics Processing Units (GPUs) to accelerate model training by parallelizing computations. PyTorch supports GPU acceleration, enabling faster training of deep learning models.
- **Early Stopping**: A regularization technique that involves monitoring model performance on a validation set during training and stopping the training process when the performance starts to degrade, preventing overfitting.

CHAPTER 8
Deployment and Productionization

Introduction

Today, Natural Language Processing (NLP) finds its applications in varied walks of life. In real-world applications, it is conducive to understanding the way from conceptualizing a model to its deployment. As practitioners, we find ourselves involved in understanding the intricacies of training models, fine-tuning hyperparameters, and achieving state-of-the-art performance on benchmark datasets. However, the ultimate test lies not just in the efficacy of our models in controlled environments but in their seamless integration into the diverse ecosystems where they are intended to operate.

This chapter deals with the transition of NLP models from research experiments to practical solutions. It discusses preparing models for deployment, navigating the deployment landscape, optimizing for performance, and ensuring ethical considerations in developing NLP models.

In this chapter, we also discuss monitoring and debugging, equipping ourselves to vigilantly observe our deployed systems, diagnose issues, and iteratively enhance their performance and reliability.

This chapter also delves into ethical considerations pertaining to the NLP technologies that rule our society. It ensures that all the NLP technologies are made with diligence and integrity, ensuring that our deployments uphold principles of fairness, transparency, and accountability.

In traversing the landscape of deployment and productionization in NLP, this chapter serves as a guide for practitioners towards the realization of impactful, responsible, and sustainable solutions that transcend the confines of research laboratories to empower and enrich the lives of individuals and communities worldwide.

Structure

In this chapter, we will discuss the following topics:

- Exporting PyTorch Models
- Deployment Strategies (Server, Edge, Cloud)
- Scaling and Performance Optimization
- Monitoring and Debugging
- Ethical Considerations in NLP

Exporting PyTorch Models

PyTorch, popular for its flexibility and ease of use in developing cutting-edge deep learning models, empowers researchers and practitioners to innovate rapidly in the domain of Natural Language Processing (NLP). However, the journey from crafting a model in PyTorch to deploying it in production environments often necessitates bridging the gap between the research and deployment ecosystems. This crucial step involves exporting PyTorch models into formats compatible with various deployment frameworks and platforms.

Exporting PyTorch models involves transforming trained models from their native PyTorch representation into formats that can be consumed by inference engines in deployment environments. This process is essential for achieving interoperability and compatibility with diverse deployment frameworks, ranging from traditional server-based setups to edge devices and cloud platforms.

Common formats for model export include Open Neural Network Exchange (ONNX) and TorchScript. ONNX, an open standard for representing deep learning models, enables interoperability between various deep learning frameworks such as PyTorch, TensorFlow, and MXNet. By exporting PyTorch models to ONNX format, practitioners unlock the ability to leverage a plethora of deployment tools and platforms that support the ONNX runtime, thereby widening the deployment horizon for their NLP solutions.

TorchScript, another versatile format for exporting PyTorch models, offers a more lightweight and efficient representation suitable for deployment scenarios where resource constraints and performance considerations are paramount. With TorchScript, PyTorch models can be serialized into a portable, optimized format that enables efficient execution across diverse hardware platforms, including CPUs, GPUs, and specialized accelerators.

It involves the conversion of dynamic computation graphs into static representations, a process crucial for achieving optimal performance and compatibility in deployment environments. This conversion, facilitated by techniques such as tracing and scripting, enables the encapsulation of model logic into a deterministic, executable form that can be efficiently executed by inference engines without relying on dynamic graph execution capabilities inherent to PyTorch.

The process of exporting PyTorch models also encompasses considerations such as handling model dependencies, preprocessing and postprocessing logic, and platform-specific optimizations to ensure seamless integration and optimal performance in deployment environments. By embracing best practices and leveraging the rich ecosystem of tools and libraries available in the PyTorch ecosystem, practitioners can streamline the process of exporting PyTorch models, paving the way for their deployment and utilization in real-world NLP applications.

Exporting PyTorch models constitutes a pivotal step in the journey of transitioning NLP solutions from research prototypes to production-ready systems. By harnessing the capabilities of formats such as ONNX and TorchScript and adopting best practices for model conversion and optimization, practitioners can unlock the full potential of their PyTorch models, empowering them to make meaningful contributions in diverse deployment environments and domains.

Deployment Strategies (Server, Edge, Cloud)

In the realm of NLP, deploying models efficiently and effectively is paramount for translating research innovations into tangible solutions that address real-world challenges. The landscape of deployment strategies encompasses options, each required to meet specific requirements, constraints, and use cases. Among these strategies, server-based deployments, edge deployments, and cloud deployments stand out as prominent paradigms, each offering unique advantages and considerations.

Server-Based Deployments

Server-based deployments involve hosting NLP models on dedicated server infrastructure, typically within data centers or cloud environments. It is also referred to as On-Premises Deployment.

Key components of Server-Based Deployments are:

- **Custom Hardware**: Depending on the complexity and scale of the NLP model, organizations may invest in high-performance hardware such as GPUs and specialized servers.
- **Security and Privacy**: Organizations retain full control over data processing, which is critical for sectors such as healthcare, finance, and government, where data privacy and security are top priorities.

- **Limited Scalability**: On-premises solutions are limited by available physical resources, requiring careful planning for scaling.

Advantages of Server-Based Deployments are:

- **Data Control**: Sensitive data remains within the organization's infrastructure, reducing the risk of security breaches.
- **Customization**: Complete flexibility to customize the infrastructure and software stack based on specific requirements.
- **Regulatory Compliance**: Meets regulatory demands for industries where data must be processed locally (for example, GDPR compliance).

Use Case Example: A healthcare provider deploying an NLP model on premises to analyze patient medical records for clinical decision support while also maintaining strict privacy requirements.

This deployment strategy is well-suited for applications requiring centralized processing, scalability, and robust computational resources. By leveraging server-based deployments, organizations can consolidate computational resources, centralize data management, and facilitate seamless access to NLP services across distributed client applications.

Key considerations in server-based deployments include:

  - Provisioning and managing server infrastructure
  - Ensuring high availability and fault tolerance
  - Optimizing resource utilization to accommodate varying workloads efficiently.
  - Data privacy and access control play a crucial role in safeguarding sensitive information processed by server-hosted NLP models.

- **Edge Deployments**: Edge deployments entail deploying NLP models directly onto edge devices, such as smartphones, IoT devices, or edge servers, enabling inference to be performed locally on the device. This decentralized deployment strategy offers advantages such as low latency, offline capability, and enhanced privacy by processing data locally without the need for continuous network connectivity.

  Edge deployments are particularly well-suited for NLP applications requiring real-time responsiveness, privacy-sensitive processing, or operation in bandwidth-constrained environments. Examples include voice assistants on smartphones, sentiment analysis in IoT devices, or language translation on edge servers in remote locations.

Challenges associated with edge deployments include resource constraints inherent to edge devices, such as limited computational power, memory, and battery life.

Optimizing NLP models for efficient inference on edge devices, minimizing model size and computational complexity, and implementing power-efficient algorithms are essential considerations in realizing effective edge deployments.

Key components of Edge Deployments include the following:

- **Edge Devices**: Devices with sufficient computational power, such as smartphones, IoT sensors, or routers, where NLP models can be deployed.
- **Model Optimization**: NLP models need to be compressed or optimized to run on edge devices due to resource constraints such as memory, processing power, and battery life.
- **Reduced Latency**: Processing happens locally, so the response time is faster, which is essential for applications requiring real-time processing.

Advantages of Edge Deployments include the following:

- **Low Latency**: Real-time processing without the need to send data over the internet, making it ideal for time-sensitive applications.
- **Data Privacy**: Since data processing happens locally, sensitive information does not need to leave the device, improving privacy.
- **Offline Functionality**: NLP models can function even in areas with poor or no internet connectivity.

Use Case Example: A smartphone app for real-time language translation that runs an NLP model on the device, allowing users to translate conversations without an internet connection.

- **Hybrid Deployment**: Hybrid deployment combines elements of both cloud-based and on-premises strategies, providing flexibility to choose where the NLP model processes data. Organizations can maintain critical or sensitive data on-premises while leveraging the cloud for less sensitive operations or for scaling up when necessary.

Key components of Hybrid Deployment include the following:

- **Data Segmentation**: Sensitive data is processed on-premises, while less sensitive operations, such as model training or inference, are handled in the cloud.
- **Cloud Bursting**: During high demand, the system can temporarily "burst" into the cloud to handle additional workloads.
- **Seamless Integration**: Ensures that on-premises systems and cloud services work together efficiently.

Advantages of Hybrid Deployment include the following:

- **Flexibility**: Combines the best of both on-premises and cloud environments, allowing for custom configurations based on data sensitivity and workload needs.

- **Cost Efficiency**: Reduces costs by leveraging the cloud for non-critical tasks while keeping sensitive data secure on-premises.
- **Scalability**: Can easily scale resources by using cloud services when needed.

Use Case Example: A financial institution processing sensitive customer data on-premises while leveraging the cloud for running large-scale NLP model training tasks to improve fraud detection.

- **Cloud Deployments**: Cloud deployments involve hosting NLP models on cloud computing platforms, such as Amazon Web Services (AWS), Google Cloud Platform (GCP), or Microsoft Azure. Cloud deployments offer scalability, flexibility, and accessibility, enabling organizations to leverage on-demand computational resources, managed services, and infrastructure-as-code capabilities for deploying and scaling NLP solutions rapidly.

  Cloud deployments are well-suited for a wide range of NLP applications, from web-based chatbots and virtual assistants to large-scale text analytics pipelines and language understanding services. By harnessing the elasticity of cloud computing, organizations can dynamically scale NLP services in response to fluctuating workloads, optimize costs through pay-per-use pricing models, and benefit from managed services for tasks such as model training, deployment, and monitoring.

  However, cloud deployments also pose challenges related to data privacy, regulatory compliance, and vendor lock-in. Organizations must carefully assess the trade-offs between the benefits of cloud computing and considerations such as data sovereignty, security, and long-term sustainability when opting for cloud-based NLP deployments.

Key components of Cloud Infrastructure include the following:

- **Cloud services** offer Infrastructure-as-a-Service (IaaS) and Platform-as-a-Service (PaaS) options, which allow organizations to host NLP models without worrying about underlying hardware management.
- **Scalability**: Cloud platforms automatically scale resources based on demand, making it easier to handle varying workloads, such as high-volume text processing tasks.
- **Pre-Trained Models**: Cloud platforms often offer NLP APIs (for example, AWS Comprehend, Google Cloud NLP) that provide pre-trained models for tasks such as text classification, named entity recognition (NER), and sentiment analysis.

Advantages:

- **Elasticity**: Easily scales up or down based on user traffic or processing needs.
- **Reduced Infrastructure Costs**: Eliminates the need for maintaining physical servers and hardware.
- **Easy Integration**: Cloud platforms provide APIs and software development kits (SDKs) that can be integrated into applications.

Use Case Example: An e-commerce platform deploying a cloud-based NLP model to analyze customer reviews in real-time and provide sentiment analysis for product feedback.

Deployment strategies in NLP provide several options, each offering unique advantages and considerations. Server-based deployments provide centralized processing and scalability; edge deployments offer low latency and privacy benefits, while cloud deployments deliver scalability, flexibility, and managed services. By understanding the strengths and trade-offs of each deployment strategy, organizations can architect NLP solutions that align with their specific requirements, constraints, and objectives, paving the way for impactful and scalable deployments in diverse application domains.

Scaling and Performance Optimization

In the domain of Natural Language Processing (NLP), the ability to scale models and optimize their performance is critical for deploying efficient and effective solutions that meet the demands of real-world applications. As NLP models continue to grow in complexity and size, scaling strategies and performance optimization techniques play a pivotal role in ensuring that models can handle large volumes of data, deliver timely responses, and operate with optimal resource utilization.

- **Scaling Strategies**: Scaling NLP models involves adapting them to handle increasing workloads, larger datasets, and diverse deployment environments. Several scaling strategies are commonly employed to address these challenges.
- **Model Parallelism**: Divide large models into smaller components and distribute computations across multiple processing units, such as GPUs or TPUs, to accelerate training and inference. Model parallelism enables efficient utilization of computational resources and facilitates scalability to handle larger models and datasets.
- **Data Parallelism**: Distribute training data across multiple processing units and synchronize model updates to accelerate training and improve throughput. Data parallelism enables parallel processing of batches across distributed systems, reducing training time and enabling efficient scaling to larger datasets.
- **Pipeline Parallelism**: Partition NLP workflows into sequential stages and distribute computations across multiple processing units, enabling overlapping

execution and reducing overall latency. Pipeline parallelism facilitates efficient resource utilization and accelerates inference by parallelizing sequential tasks.

- **Distributed Training**: Distribute training across multiple machines or clusters to accelerate convergence and handle large-scale datasets. Distributed training frameworks, such as TensorFlow's Distributed Strategy and PyTorch's `DistributedDataParallel`, enable seamless scaling of NLP models across distributed environments.
- **Performance Optimization Techniques**: Optimizing the performance of NLP models involves enhancing efficiency, reducing latency, and minimizing resource consumption without compromising accuracy or functionality. Several performance optimization techniques are commonly employed to achieve these objectives.
- **Quantization**: Convert model parameters from high precision (for example, 32-bit floating-point) to lower precision (for example, 8-bit integers) to reduce memory footprint and accelerate inference. Quantization techniques, such as post-training quantization and quantization-aware training, enable efficient deployment of NLP models on resource-constrained devices.
- **Pruning**: Identify and remove redundant or insignificant parameters from NLP models to reduce model size, improve inference speed, and minimize computational overhead. Pruning techniques, such as magnitude-based pruning and structured pruning, enable efficient model compression without sacrificing performance.
- **Kernel Optimization**: Optimize low-level operations and kernel implementations to leverage hardware-specific optimizations, such as Single Instruction, Multiple Data (SIMD) instructions and hardware accelerators (for example, CUDA for GPUs). Kernel optimization techniques enable efficient utilization of hardware resources and accelerate computation in NLP models.
- **Caching and Memorization**: Cache intermediate computations and results to avoid redundant computations and improve inference speed. Memorization techniques enable efficient reuse of previously computed results, reducing computational overhead and latency in NLP applications.
- **Asynchronous Inference**: Parallelize inference requests and process them asynchronously to reduce latency and improve throughput in NLP inference pipelines. Asynchronous inference techniques enable efficient utilization of computational resources and facilitate real-time processing of incoming requests.

By leveraging scaling strategies and performance optimization techniques, organizations can deploy NLP solutions that are scalable, efficient, and responsive to the demands of real-world applications. From distributed training and model parallelism to quantization and kernel optimization, these techniques enable practitioners to unlock the full potential of NLP models and deliver impactful solutions that meet the needs of diverse deployment environments and use cases.

Monitoring and Debugging

In the field of NLP, where models continuously interact with vast volumes of textual data in real-time applications, effective monitoring and debugging practices are important for ensuring the reliability, performance, and integrity of deployed NLP systems. Monitoring enables practitioners to gain insights into the behavior and performance of NLP models in production environments, while debugging facilitates the identification and resolution of issues and anomalies that may arise during deployment.

Key components of Monitoring and Debugging in NLP are:

- **Logging and Metrics Collection**: Implement comprehensive logging mechanisms to capture relevant information, such as input data, model predictions, inference times, and error rates, during the execution of NLP workflows. Additionally, collect performance metrics, such as throughput, latency, and resource utilization, to monitor the overall health and efficiency of deployed NLP systems.
- **Alerting and Anomaly Detection**: Set up alerting mechanisms to notify stakeholders of deviations from expected behavior or performance thresholds in deployed NLP systems. Implement anomaly detection algorithms to automatically identify and flag unusual patterns or outliers in input data, model predictions, or system metrics, enabling proactive intervention and troubleshooting.
- **Visualization and Dashboards**: Visualize monitoring data and metrics using interactive dashboards and visualization tools to facilitate real-time analysis and exploration of system behavior and performance trends. Dashboards provide stakeholders with intuitive insights into the operational status, efficiency, and effectiveness of deployed NLP systems, enabling informed decision-making and troubleshooting.
- **Profiling and Performance Analysis**: Conduct profiling and performance analysis of NLP workflows to identify bottlenecks, inefficiencies, and performance hotspots that may impact system responsiveness and scalability. Profile code execution, memory usage, and I/O operations to pinpoint areas for optimization and improvement in deployed NLP systems.
- **Root Cause Analysis**: Perform root cause analysis to identify the underlying causes of issues, errors, or anomalies observed in deployed NLP systems. Use techniques such as log analysis, stack traces, and hypothesis testing to diagnose and debug issues effectively, tracing them back to their origins in the system architecture, codebase, or data pipeline.

Best practices for Monitoring and Debugging in NLP include the following:

- **Proactive Monitoring**: Continuously monitor the health, performance, and behavior of deployed NLP systems in real-time, proactively detecting and addressing issues before they escalate and impact users or stakeholders.
- **Granular Logging**: Log detailed information at each stage of the NLP workflow, including input data, preprocessing steps, model predictions, and postprocessing operations, to facilitate traceability and debugging of issues across the entire pipeline.
- **Automated Testing**: Implement automated testing frameworks and regression tests to validate the correctness and robustness of NLP models and pipelines across different input scenarios, edge cases, and deployment environments.
- **Continuous Integration and Deployment (CI/CD)**: Integrate monitoring and debugging practices into CI/CD pipelines to automate the deployment, testing, and validation of changes to NLP systems, ensuring consistency, reliability, and quality across software releases.
- **Collaborative Debugging**: Foster a collaborative environment where interdisciplinary teams, including data scientists, engineers, and domain experts, collaborate closely to diagnose and debug issues in deployed NLP systems, leveraging their collective expertise and insights.
- **Feedback Loop**: Establish a feedback loop between monitoring, debugging, and model refinement processes, enabling continuous improvement and optimization of NLP systems based on real-world observations and user feedback.

By adopting the aforementioned proactive approach for monitoring and debugging, organizations can ensure the reliability, performance, and effectiveness of deployed NLP systems in diverse real-world applications and environments.

Ethical Considerations in NLP

Ethical considerations in NLP are often accompanied by bias and fairness, privacy and data protection, transparency and accountability, security concerns, social impact, and ethical AI development, which are described in *Figure* 8.1.

Bias and Fairness

- **Data Bias**: Datasets used in training NLP models often contain biases reflecting societal prejudices. This can lead to models that perpetuate and even amplify these biases.
- **Algorithmic Bias**: Even if data is unbiased, algorithms themselves can introduce or amplify biases.

- **Mitigation Strategies**: Techniques such as bias detection, debiasing algorithms, and diverse training data can help mitigate these issues.

Privacy and Data Protection

- **Data Collection**: Ensuring that data is collected ethically, with informed consent from individuals.
- **Anonymization**: Techniques to anonymize data to protect user identity, while maintaining data utility.
- **Regulations**: Compliance with legal frameworks such as the General Data Protection Regulation (GDPR) and California Consumer Privacy Act (CCPA).

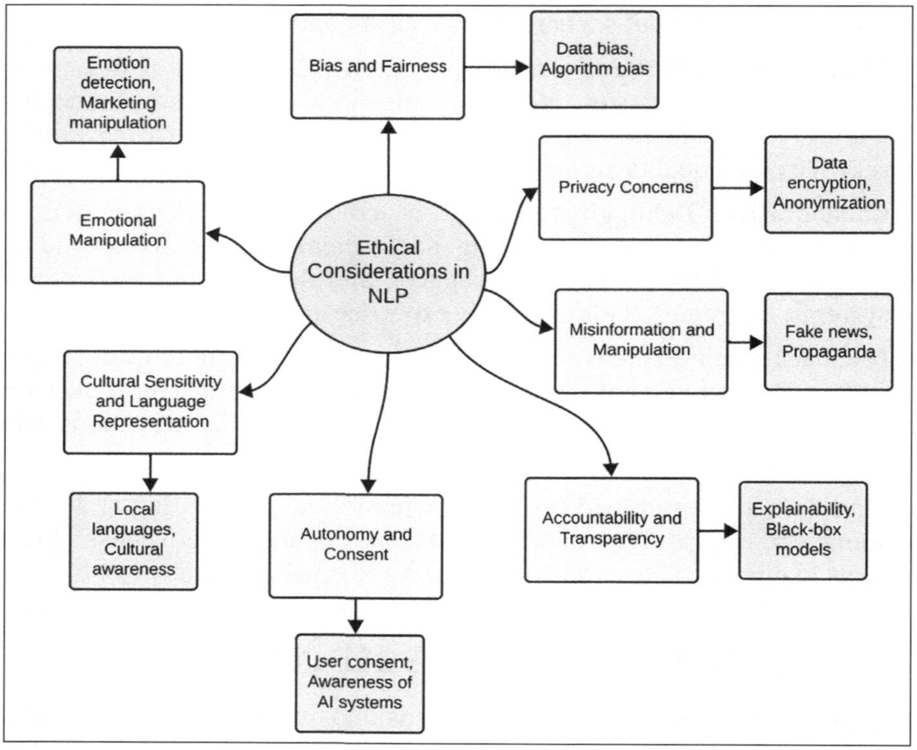

Figure 8.1: *Ethical Considerations in* NLP

Transparency and Accountability

- **Explainability**: Developing models that provide understandable explanations for their decisions and outputs.
- **Accountability**: Establishing clear lines of accountability for decisions made by NLP systems, including error analysis and responsibility for mistakes.
- **Auditing**: Regular audits of NLP systems to ensure they meet ethical standards and regulations.

Security Concerns

- **Adversarial Attacks**: Protecting NLP systems from malicious inputs designed to deceive or disrupt them.
- **Robustness**: Building robust models that can withstand unexpected or manipulated inputs.
- **Data Security**: Ensuring that the data used and produced by NLP systems is stored and transmitted securely.

Social Impact

- **Disinformation**: Addressing the role of NLP in spreading fake news and misinformation.
- **Manipulation**: Preventing the use of NLP for manipulative purposes, such as automated propaganda or social engineering.
- **Accessibility**: Ensuring that NLP technologies are accessible and beneficial to a broad audience, including marginalized communities.

Ethical AI Development

- **Human-Centric Design**: Designing NLP systems that prioritize human values and societal well-being.
- **Interdisciplinary Collaboration**: Working with ethicists, sociologists, and other experts to understand the broader implications of NLP technologies.
- **Sustainable AI:** Considering the environmental impact of NLP models, particularly large-scale models that require significant computational resources.

Conclusion

In this chapter, we explored crucial aspects of deploying and optimizing NLP models using PyTorch. We discussed various methods of exporting PyTorch models, ensuring they can seamlessly transition from research to deployment environments. We also discussed deployment strategies—whether on servers, at the edge, or in the cloud—provide flexibility in meeting diverse application needs, from real-time inference to resource-constrained environments.

Monitoring and debugging strategies were discussed to maintain model robustness and reliability throughout its operational lifecycle, emphasizing the importance of continuous evaluation and iteration.

Ethical considerations have also been discussed, urging practitioners to prioritize transparency, fairness, and privacy in NLP applications. So, ethical frameworks and responsible AI practices serve as guiding principles to mitigate biases and uphold societal values.

In the next chapter, we will discuss Sentiment Analysis on Social Media Data, Text Classification for News Articles, Chatbot Development with PyTorch, Neural Machine Translation System, and Question Answering System.

Points to Remember

- Use **`torch.jit`** for exporting models to a format suitable for deployment.
- Optimize models for specific deployment environments using techniques such as model quantization and size reduction.
- Establish comprehensive monitoring systems to track model performance, data drift, and potential biases in real-world deployments.
- Implement debugging tools and techniques to diagnose and resolve issues during development and deployment phases.
- Prioritize fairness, transparency, and accountability in NLP model development and deployment.
- Mitigate biases and uphold privacy standards to ensure the ethical use of NLP technologies.
- Engage stakeholders and consider societal impacts when designing and deploying NLP solutions.
- Strive for responsible AI practices to foster trust and acceptance of NLP technologies in broader society.

Multiple Choice Questions

1. Which of the following techniques is recommended for exporting PyTorch models for deployment?
   a. `torch.save()`
   b. `torch.onnx.export()`
   c. `model.export_to_file()`
   d. `torch.tensor.export()`
2. When considering deployment strategies for NLP models, what factors should influence the choice between server-side, edge, or cloud deployment?
   a. Model training time
   b. Model complexity
   c. Latency requirements
   d. All of the above

3. Which technique is used to improve the performance of NLP models by reducing their memory footprint and inference time?
    a. Model serialization
    b. Data augmentation
    c. Model quantization
    d. Gradient clipping
4. What is a recommended approach for monitoring deployed NLP models to ensure their continued reliability and performance?
    a. Use `print()` statements in the inference code
    b. Implement comprehensive logging and metrics tracking
    c. Conduct manual checks on a periodic basis
    d. Ignore monitoring after initial deployment
5. In the context of ethical considerations in NLP, what does transparency refer to?
    a. Making the model code publicly available
    b. Clearly documenting model limitations and biases
    c. Encrypting sensitive data during training
    d. Only using open-source datasets
6. Which practice helps mitigate biases in NLP models during development and deployment?
    a. Only using datasets from a single source
    b. Regularly updating model weights without retraining
    c. Conducting bias analysis on training data
    d. Avoiding diverse perspectives in data collection

Answers

1. b
2. d
3. c
4. b

5. b
6. c

Questions

1. Describe the process of exporting a PyTorch model for deployment. What are the key considerations during this process?
2. Compare and contrast server-side, edge, and cloud deployment strategies for NLP models. In what scenarios would each strategy be most suitable?
3. What are some common techniques used to optimize the performance of NLP models deployed in resource-constrained environments? Provide examples of each technique.
4. Discuss the significance of monitoring and debugging in the context of deploying NLP models. What tools and strategies can be employed for effective monitoring and debugging?
5. Why is model quantization important in the deployment of NLP models? How does it impact model performance and efficiency?
6. Explain the ethical considerations that should be taken into account when developing and deploying NLP models. How can these considerations be integrated into the development lifecycle?
7. What role does transparency play in the ethical deployment of NLP models? Provide examples of how transparency can be achieved in practice.
8. How can biases in NLP models impact their performance and fairness? What steps can be taken to identify and mitigate biases during model development and deployment?
9. Discuss the challenges and strategies associated with scaling NLP models to handle large datasets and high-throughput applications.
10. How can continuous evaluation and iteration contribute to the long-term success of deployed NLP models? Provide examples of metrics and criteria used for evaluation.

Key Terms

- **PyTorch Models Exporting**: The process of converting PyTorch models into formats suitable for deployment, such as ONNX or TorchScript.
- **Deployment Strategies**: Approaches for deploying NLP models in various environments, including server-side, edge devices, and cloud platforms.

- **Model Quantization**: Technique to reduce the precision of numerical values in models to improve efficiency without sacrificing much accuracy.
- **Performance Optimization**: Methods to enhance the speed and efficiency of NLP models, including parallelism, pruning, and optimization algorithms.
- **Monitoring and Debugging**: Practices for tracking model performance and diagnosing issues during deployment to ensure reliability and effectiveness.
- **Ethical Considerations**: Principles and guidelines addressing fairness, transparency, privacy, and accountability in the development and deployment of NLP models.
- **Bias Mitigation**: Techniques to identify and mitigate biases in NLP models to ensure equitable and unbiased outcomes.
- **Model Scaling**: Processes and techniques for scaling NLP models to handle larger datasets and higher computational demands.
- **Continuous Evaluation**: Ongoing assessment of deployed models to monitor performance metrics, detect drift, and guide iterative improvements.
- **Responsible AI**: Practices and frameworks for designing and deploying AI systems, including NLP models, that prioritize ethical considerations and societal impact.

CHAPTER 9
Case Studies and Practical Examples

Introduction

In the field of Natural Language Processing (NLP), there are numerous practical applications and real-world case studies that describe how theoretical concepts are applied to solve complex problems. Sentiment analysis is one of the important applications of NLP that involves retrieving and analyzing information from given data and extracting emotions or sentiments expressed by users. Multilingual NLP and cross-lingual transfer learning allow models trained on one language to be adapted for use in other languages, significantly reducing the need for extensive language-specific data.

This chapter discusses techniques for building multilingual models and explores how PyTorch facilitates cross-lingual transfer learning, enabling NLP applications to reach a global audience. Explainable AI in NLP is crucial so as to have transparency and trust in the models to be developed. The convergence of NLP and computer vision opens up new possibilities for creating systems that can understand and interpret both text and visual information.

This chapter explores case studies where NLP and computer vision are combined using PyTorch. In the field of NLP, Reinforcement Learning (RL) is used for optimizing dialogue systems to improve machine translation. RL offers a dynamic approach to enhancing NLP models. In this section, we delve into how reinforcement learning can be applied to NLP tasks using PyTorch.

By examining these case studies and practical examples, this chapter aims to provide a comprehensive overview of how NLP techniques can be applied to address real-world problems. Through the lens of PyTorch, we not only explore the implementation details but also highlight the broader implications and potential of these cutting-edge NLP applications.

Structure

In this chapter, we will discuss the following topics:

- Sentiment Analysis on Social Media Data
- Text Classification for News Articles
- Chatbot Development with PyTorch
- Neural Machine Translation System
- Question Answering Systems

Sentiment Analysis on Social Media Data

The advent of social media platforms has revolutionized the way people communicate, share opinions, and interact with the world. These platforms generate an enormous volume of unstructured textual data, offering numerous insights into public sentiment and opinion. Sentiment analysis, also known as opinion mining, is a vital application of NLP that focuses on identifying and extracting subjective information from this textual data. By understanding the sentiment expressed in social media posts, businesses, researchers, and policymakers can make informed decisions and respond effectively to public opinion.

Sentiment analysis on social media data is conducive due to the following reasons:

- **Business Intelligence**: Companies can know customer satisfaction, monitor brand reputation, and identify market trends by analyzing customer feedback and reviews.
- **Public Opinion**: Governments and organizations can understand public sentiment on various issues, enabling them to make data-driven decisions.
- **Marketing and Advertising**: Targeted marketing campaigns can be designed based on the sentiment of potential customers, improving engagement and conversion rates.
- **Crisis Management**: By monitoring social media for negative sentiment, organizations can quickly address issues and mitigate potential PR crises.

Challenges in Sentiment Analysis

Despite its importance, sentiment analysis on social media data presents several challenges:

- **Variety of Expressions**: People express sentiments in diverse ways, using slang, abbreviations, emojis, and mixed languages, making it difficult to standardize and analyze the text.

- **Context Dependence:** The sentiment of a phrase can depend heavily on its context. For example, the word "*great*" can be positive in one context but sarcastic in another.
- **Noise and Irrelevance:** Social media data often contains noise, such as irrelevant posts, spam, and advertisements, which can affect the accuracy of sentiment analysis.
- **Dynamic Language:** Language on social media evolves rapidly, with new words, phrases, and memes constantly emerging, requiring models to adapt quickly.

The following steps outline the process of developing a sentiment analysis model using PyTorch:

1. **Data Collection and Preprocessing:**

   Data Collection: Gather social media data using APIs from platforms such as Twitter, Facebook, or Instagram.

   Preprocessing involves the following steps:

   a. **Text Cleaning**: Remove noise such as URLs, mentions, hashtags, and special characters.

   b. **Tokenization:** Split the text into tokens (words or subwords) for further processing.

   c. **Normalization**: Convert text to lowercase, handle contractions, and perform stemming or lemmatization.

2. **Embedding Layer:**

   a. **Word Embeddings:** Use pre-trained word embeddings (for example, GloVe, Word2Vec) or train embeddings on your dataset to convert tokens into dense vectors.

   b. **Embedding Layer:** Implement an embedding layer in PyTorch to map tokens to their corresponding embedding vectors.

3. **Model Architecture:**

   a. **Recurrent Neural Networks (RNNs):** Utilize RNNs, LSTMs, or GRUs to capture sequential dependencies in the text.

   b. **Attention Mechanisms:** Incorporate attention mechanisms to focus on important parts of the text.

   c. **Transformers:** Use transformer-based models such as BERT for their superior performance in capturing contextual information.

4. **Training and Evaluation:**

    a. **Loss Function:** Choose an appropriate loss function, such as binary cross-entropy for binary sentiment classification or categorical cross-entropy for multi-class classification.

    b. **Optimization**: Use optimizers, namely Adam or SGD, to train the model.

    c. **Evaluation Metrics:** Evaluate the model using metrics such as accuracy, precision, recall, and F1-score.

5. **Fine-Tuning and Deployment:**

    a. **Hyperparameter Tuning:** Experiment with different hyperparameters to optimize model performance.

    b. **Model Deployment**: Deploy the trained model as an API or integrate it into an application for real-time sentiment analysis.

Example: Sentiment Analysis with PyTorch

Here is a simplified example of building a sentiment analysis model using PyTorch:

```
import torch
import torch.nn as nn
import torch.optim as optim
from torchtext.data import Field, LabelField, TabularDataset,
BucketIterator

# Define Fields
TEXT = Field(tokenize='spacy', tokenizer_language='en_core_web_sm')
LABEL = LabelField(dtype=torch.float)

# Load Dataset
train_data, test_data = TabularDataset.splits(
    path='data',
    train='train.csv',
    test='test.csv',
    format='csv',
    fields=[('text', TEXT), ('label', LABEL)]
)

# Build Vocabulary
TEXT.build_vocab(train_data, max_size=25000)
LABEL.build_vocab(train_data)

# Create Iterators
train_iterator, test_iterator = BucketIterator.splits(
    (train_data, test_data),
```

```
    batch_size=64,
    device=torch.device('cuda' if torch.cuda.is_available() else 'cpu')
)

# Define Model
class SentimentRNN(nn.Module):
    def __init__(self, input_dim, embedding_dim, hidden_dim, output_
dim):
        super(SentimentRNN, self).__init__()
        self.embedding = nn.Embedding(input_dim, embedding_dim)
        self.rnn = nn.LSTM(embedding_dim, hidden_dim)
        self.fc = nn.Linear(hidden_dim, output_dim)

    def forward(self, text):
        embedded = self.embedding(text)
        output, (hidden, cell) = self.rnn(embedded)
        return self.fc(hidden.squeeze(0))

# Initialize Model
input_dim = len(TEXT.vocab)
embedding_dim = 100
hidden_dim = 256
output_dim = 1

model = SentimentRNN(input_dim, embedding_dim, hidden_dim, output_dim)

# Train Model
optimizer = optim.Adam(model.parameters())
criterion = nn.BCEWithLogitsLoss()

# Training Loop
for epoch in range(10):
    for batch in train_iterator:
        optimizer.zero_grad()
        predictions = model(batch.text).squeeze(1)
        loss = criterion(predictions, batch.label)
        loss.backward()
        optimizer.step()
```

In this example, we have defined a simple RNN-based sentiment analysis model using PyTorch. The model consists of an embedding layer, an LSTM layer, and a fully connected layer for binary classification. We use torchtext to handle data preprocessing and batch creation, making the implementation more streamlined and efficient.

Sentiment analysis on social media data is a powerful tool for extracting valuable insights from the vast amount of user-generated content available online. Through continuous advancements in NLP techniques and tools, the potential for sentiment analysis to drive impactful outcomes will continue to grow.

Text Classification For News Articles

Text classification is a fundamental task in Natural Language Processing (NLP) that involves categorizing text into predefined categories. One of the most common applications of text classification is categorizing news articles into topics such as politics, sports, technology, and entertainment.

The following example uses a dataset from the Hugging Face Datasets library:

```
!pip install transformers
import pandas as pd
import numpy as np
import requests
import seaborn as sns
import matplotlib.pyplot as plt
import nltk

from transformers import BertTokenizer, BertForSequenceClassification
from torch.utils.data import TensorDataset, DataLoader

nltk.download('stopwords')
nltk.download('punkt')
!pip install datasets
from datasets import load_dataset

# loading the "fake_news_english" dataset from Huggingface
dataset = load_dataset("fake_news_english")
train_data = dataset["train"]

## Converting  training dataset intc a dataframe
df = pd.DataFrame.from_dict(dataset['train'])

df.head()
```

article_number	url_of_article	fake_or_satire	url_of_rebutting_article	
0	375	http://www.redflagnews.com/headlines-2016/cdc-...	1	http://www.snopes.com/cdc-forced-vaccinations/

1	376	http://www.redflagnews.com/headlines-2016/-out...	1	http://www.snopes.com/white-house-logo-change/
2	377	http://www.redflagnews.com/headlines-2016/whit...	1	http://www.snopes.com/obama-veterans-money-to-...
3	378	http://www.redflagnews.com/headlines-2016/obam...	1	http://www.snopes.com/obama-veterans-money-to-...
4	379	http://www.redflagnews.com/headlines-2016/cali...	1	http://www.snopes.com/california-to-jail-clima...

```
print(df.info())
print(df.describe())
print(df.shape)

<class 'pandas.core.frame.DataFrame'>
RangeIndex: 492 entries, 0 to 491
Data columns (total 4 columns):
 #   Column                  Non-Null Count  Dtype
---  ------                  --------------  -----
 0   article_number          492 non-null    int64
 1   url_of_article          492 non-null    object
 2   fake_or_satire          492 non-null    int64
 3   url_of_rebutting_article 492 non-null    object
dtypes: int64(2), object(2)
memory usage: 15.5+ KB
None
       article_number  fake_or_satire
count      492.000000      492.000000
mean       289.792683        0.591463
std        169.817410        0.492064
min          2.000000        0.000000
25%        138.750000        0.000000
50%        296.500000        1.000000
75%        432.250000        1.000000
max        595.000000        1.000000
(492, 4)


## looping  through URLs in dataframe
```

```
for url in df['url_of_rebutting_article']:
    try:
          ## creates Article object and download/parse HTML content
        article = Article(url)
        article.download()
        article.parse()

          ## extracts title and main article text using newspaper3k
        title = article.title
        text = article.text

          ## appends extracted data to lists
        title_list.append(title)
        text_list.append(text)

      ## checks for specific types of exceptions that may be raised
    except requests.exceptions.HTTPError as errh:
        print("HTTP Error:", errh)
    except requests.exceptions.ConnectionError as errc:
        print("Error Connecting:", errc)
    except requests.exceptions.Timeout as errt:
        print("Timeout Error:", errt)
    except requests.exceptions.RequestException as err:
        print("Something went wrong:", err)
    except:
        print("An error occurred while processing the URL:", url)

  # creates new dataframe with scraped data
new_df = pd.DataFrame({'title': title_list, 'text': text_list})
new_df = new_df['title']+new_df['text']

## Renaming columns, Dropping duplicates and Unwanted columns
df.rename(columns = {'fake_or_satire': 'labels'}, inplace = True)

df = df.drop(['article_number', 'url_of_article', 'url_of_rebutting_
article'], axis = 1)
df ## displaying dataframe
```

labels	
0	1
1	1
2	1
3	1

4	1
...	...
487	0
488	0
489	0
490	0
491	0

492 rows × 1 column

```
df[df['labels'] == 0].info()
df[df['labels'] == 1].info()

<class 'pandas.core.frame.DataFrame'>
Int64Index: 201 entries, 291 to 491
Data columns (total 1 columns):
 #   Column  Non-Null Count  Dtype
---  ------  --------------  -----
 0   labels  201 non-null    int64
dtypes: int64(1)
memory usage: 3.1 KB
<class 'pandas.core.frame.DataFrame'>
Int64Index: 291 entries, 0 to 290
Data columns (total 1 columns):
 #   Column  Non-Null Count  Dtype
---  ------  --------------  -----
 0   labels  291 non-null    int64
dtypes: int64(1)
memory usage: 4.5 KB


sns.countplot(y='labels', palette="coolwarm", data=df).set_title
('Distribution of true or fake news')
plt.show()
```

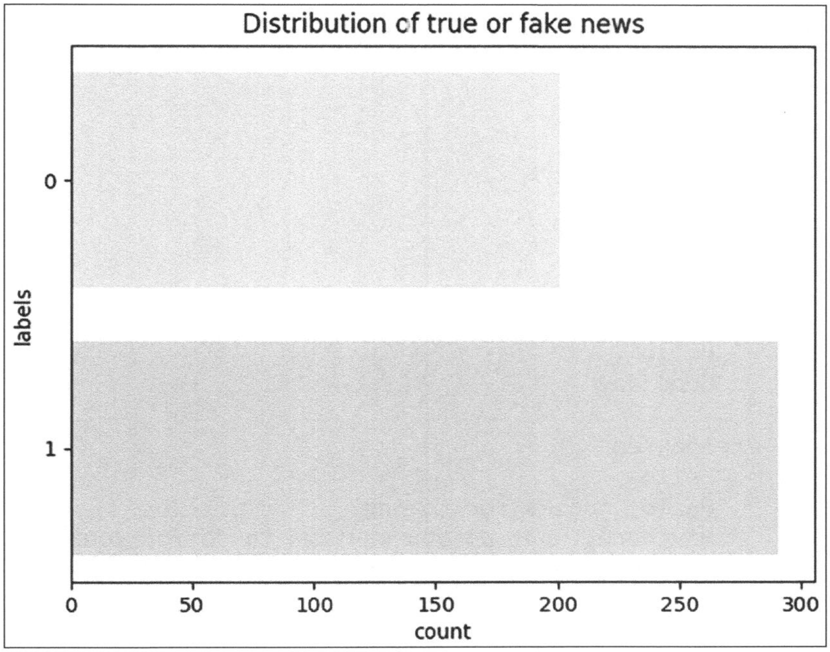

***Figure 9.1**: Distribution of true or fake news*

In the preceding example, we have preprocessed the dataset, split the dataset into training and testing data, and performed fake news classification on it.

Chatbot Development with PyTorch

Chatbots have revolutionized customer service, providing instant support and engagement across various industries. Developing a chatbot involves several steps, from data collection and preprocessing to designing and training conversational models. In this section, we will guide you through building a chatbot using PyTorch, focusing on the key components and processes involved.

The goal is to create a chatbot capable of understanding user inputs and generating appropriate responses. For this example, we will build a simple rule-based conversational agent that can handle basic queries about a company's services.

- **Dataset:** We will use a custom dataset comprising pairs of questions and answers. This dataset simulates typical interactions a customer might have with a company's support chatbot.
- **Data Preprocessing:** Data preprocessing involves tokenizing the text, creating vocabulary, and converting words into numerical representations. We will use the NLTK library for tokenization and build a vocabulary from the dataset.

The **dataset.json** file may comprise the following contents:

```
{
  "intents": [
    {
      "tag": "greeting",
      "patterns": [
        "Hi",
        "Hey",
        "How are you",
        "Is anyone there?",
        "Hello",
        "Good day"
      ],
      "responses": [
        "Hello",
        "Hello, thanks for coming",
        "Hi there, what do you want me to do for you?",
        "Hi there, how can I help?"
      ]
    },
    ...
  ]
}
```

```
import json
import nltk
import numpy as np
from nltk.tokenize import word_tokenize
from sklearn.preprocessing import LabelEncoder

# Load the dataset
with open('chatbot_dataset.json') as file:
    data = json.load(file)

# Tokenize the sentences
nltk.download('punkt')
all_words = []
tags = []
xy = []
for intent in data['intents']:
    for pattern in intent['patterns']:
        w = word_tokenize(pattern)
        all_words.extend(w)
        xy.append((w, intent['tag']))
    tags.append(intent['tag'])
```

```
# Create vocabulary and label encoder
all_words = sorted(set(all_words))
tags = sorted(set(tags))
label_encoder = LabelEncoder()
labels = label_encoder.fit_transform(tags)

# Convert words to numerical representations
X_train = []
y_train = []
for (pattern_sentence, tag) in xy:
    bag = [1 if w in pattern_sentence else 0 for w in all_words]
    X_train.append(bag)
    y_train.append(label_encoder.transform([tag])[0])

X_train = np.array(X_train)
y_train = np.array(y_train)
```

- **Model Architecture:** We will use a simple feedforward neural network for this task. The network will take the bag-of-words representation of the input sentence and output the probability distribution over the possible tags.

```
import torch
import torch.nn as nn
import torch.optim as optim
from torch.utils.data import DataLoader, TensorDataset

# Convert data to PyTorch tensors
X_train = torch.tensor(X_train, dtype=torch.float32)
y_train = torch.tensor(y_train, dtype=torch.long)

# Create DataLoader
train_dataset = TensorDataset(X_train, y_train)
train_loader = DataLoader(train_dataset, batch_size=8,
shuffle=True)

# Define the model
class ChatbotModel(nn.Module):
    def __init__(self, input_size, hidden_size, output_size):
        super(ChatbotModel, self).__init__()
        self.fc1 = nn.Linear(input_size, hidden_size)
        self.fc2 = nn.Linear(hidden_size, output_size)

    def forward(self, x):
        x = torch.relu(self.fc1(x))
        x = self.fc2(x)
        return x
```

```
input_size = len(all_words)
hidden_size = 8
output_size = len(tags)
model = ChatbotModel(input_size, hidden_size, output_size)
```

- **Training the Model:** We will use cross-entropy loss and the Adam optimizer to train our model. The training loop will involve forward propagation, loss calculation, backpropagation, and updating the model parameters.

```
# Define loss and optimizer
criterion = nn.CrossEntropyLoss()
optimizer = optim.Adam(model.parameters(), lr=0.001)

# Training loop
num_epochs = 1000
for epoch in range(num_epochs):
    for (X_batch, y_batch) in train_loader:
        optimizer.zero_grad()
        outputs = model(X_batch)
        loss = criterion(outputs, y_batch)
        loss.backward()
        optimizer.step()
    if (epoch+1) % 100 == 0:
        print(f'Epoch {epoch+1}/{num_epochs}, Loss: {loss.
item():.4f}')
```

- **Inference:** After training the model, we can use it to predict the tag for a given user input and generate a response based on the predicted tag.

```
# Define a function to predict the tag and generate a response
def predict_class(sentence, model):
    sentence = word_tokenize(sentence)
    bag = [1 if w in sentence else 0 for w in all_words]
    X = torch.tensor(bag, dtype=torch.float32).unsqueeze(0)
    output = model(X)
    _, predicted = torch.max(output, 1)
    tag = label_encoder.inverse_transform([predicted.item()])[0]
    return tag

def get_response(tag, data):
    for intent in data['intents']:
        if intent['tag'] == tag:
            return np.random.choice(intent['responses'])

# Example usage
user_input = "How can I reset my password?"
predicted_tag = predict_class(user_input, model)
```

```
    response = get_response(predicted_tag, data)
    print(f"Bot: {response}")
```

We demonstrated how to build a simple chatbot using PyTorch. We covered data preprocessing, model architecture, training, and inference. By following these steps, you can create a basic rule-based conversational agent capable of handling simple queries, showcasing the practical application of NLP techniques using PyTorch. For more advanced chatbots, consider using more sophisticated models such as transformers or integrating with external APIs for richer interactions.

Neural Machine Translation System

Neural Machine Translation (NMT) has transformed the field of machine translation by leveraging deep learning techniques to translate text from one language to another. Unlike traditional statistical methods, NMT models can capture complex language patterns and generate more fluent and accurate translations. In this section, we will explore the development of an NMT system using PyTorch, focusing on data preprocessing, model architecture, training, and evaluation.

NMT refers to the use of deep learning models to automatically translate text from one language to another.

It is one of the popular machine translations due to its ability to handle complex linguistic structures and generate fluent translations. One popular framework for implementing NMT is PyTorch, which provides a flexible and efficient platform for building deep learning models.

Key concepts in NMT:

- **Sequence-to-Sequence Models (Seq2Seq)**: NMT systems may be implemented using neural networks called sequence-to-sequence (Seq2Seq) models. These models are designed to handle input and output sequences of variable lengths, making them ideal for tasks such as translation, where the length of the source and target sentences can vary. Seq2Seq model consists of two main components:
    - **Encoder**: The encoder reads the input sentence in the source language and converts it into a fixed-size context vector. This context vector captures the meaning of the input sentence in a condensed form.
    - **Decoder**: The decoder takes the context vector and generates the translated sentence in the target language, one word at a time.
- **Attention Mechanism**: A major improvement to Seq2Seq models is the attention mechanism. Instead of relying on a single context vector, the attention mechanism allows the model to focus on different parts of the input sentence at each decoding step. This is particularly useful for longer sentences

where a single context vector might not adequately represent all the relevant information.

- **Transformer Models**: Transformers are a newer and highly effective architecture that has revolutionized the field of NMT. Unlike traditional Seq2Seq models, which rely on recurrent neural networks (RNNs) or long short-term memory (LSTM) networks, transformers use self-attention mechanisms to process input sequences in parallel. This makes transformers faster to train and more efficient at handling long-range dependencies in the data.
- **Training Process**: The training of an NMT model typically involves minimizing the difference between the predicted translation and the actual translation using a loss function such as cross-entropy. During training, the model learns to map the source language sequence to the target language sequence by adjusting the weights of the network to reduce this error.
- **Evaluation Metrics**: To assess the quality of a neural machine translation model, various metrics are used:
    - **Bilingual Evaluation Understudy (BLEU)**: A popular metric that compares the overlap of n-grams between the generated translation and a reference translation.
    - **METEOR and TER**: Other metrics that take into account synonyms and word reordering.

A basic pipeline for NMT in PyTorch typically involves:

1. **Data Preparation**: Tokenize and preprocess the source and target languages.
2. **Model Definition**: Define the architecture (for example, Seq2Seq, Transformer).
3. **Training**: Train the model by feeding in source sentences and teaching it to predict the corresponding target sentences.
4. **Inference**: Once trained, the model can generate translations for unseen sentences.

Challenges and Future Directions:

- **Data Requirements**: Neural machine translation systems require large parallel corpora (that is, aligned sentences in both source and target languages). For many low-resource languages, these corpora are scarce, which limits the performance of NMT systems.
- **Handling Out-of-Vocabulary Words**: Even though models are trained on large vocabularies, they can still struggle with words not seen during training. Techniques such as subword tokenization (for example, Byte Pair Encoding or SentencePiece) are commonly used to address this.

- **Generalization**: NMT models sometimes struggle with generalizing to unseen sentence structures or out-of-domain text.
- **Efficiency**: Transformer models, while powerful, are computationally expensive, especially for very large datasets.

Question Answering System

Question Answering (QA) systems have become a significant component of modern AI applications, enabling machines to understand and respond to user queries based on a given context or dataset. These systems are used in various applications, such as virtual assistants, customer support, and information retrieval.

To build a QA system using PyTorch, we need to follow these general steps:

1. **Define the Problem Scope**: Determine if you are building an extractive QA system (where the answer is a segment from a given context) or a generative QA system (where the answer is generated without directly referencing the context).
2. **Dataset Collection and Preprocessing**: Popular datasets for QA include SQuAD, Natural Questions, or custom domain-specific datasets. Tokenize the questions and answers using tokenizers such as BERT's tokenizer or any other suitable tokenization method. Convert the questions and contexts into a format that the model can process (for example, padding, truncation, and attention masks). Split data into training, validation, and test sets.
3. **Select a Pre-trained Model**: Use a pre-trained language model, such as BERT, RoBERTa, or T5, from the Hugging Face `transformers` library or similar. Fine-tune the pre-trained model on your QA dataset. These models come with prebuilt architectures for token classification or sequence-to-sequence tasks.
4. **Model Architecture**: Use a model, namely BERT, with a classification head on top. The goal is to predict the start and end positions of the answer in the given context. The model should output two probability distributions, one for the start and one for the end of the answer span.
5. **Fine-Tuning the Model**: Fine-tune the model on your QA dataset. Fine-tuning typically involves adjusting hyperparameters such as learning rate, batch size, and the number of epochs.
6. **Model Evaluation**: Evaluate the model using metrics such as F1 score, Exact Match (EM), and BLEU score for generative models.
7. **Inference**: During inference, provide the model with a question and context, and get the answer.

By following the aforementioned steps, we can build a question answering system using PyTorch that leverages the power of pretrained models and fine-tuning for domain-specific performance.

Conclusion

In this chapter, we explored various practical applications of NLP using PyTorch, delving into the development of sophisticated systems that can perform specific NLP tasks. We covered a range of case studies and examples, including Sentiment Analysis on social media data, Text Classification for news articles, Chatbot Development, Neural Machine Translation, and Question Answering systems.

For each application, we walked through the essential steps: data preprocessing, model architecture, training, and evaluation. We demonstrated the use of powerful transformer models such as BERT, which have significantly advanced the field of NLP by providing state-of-the-art performance across various benchmarks.

We showed how to build a model that can understand and classify the sentiment of social media posts, a crucial task for businesses seeking to gauge public opinion. We also discussed how to categorize news articles into predefined topics, highlighting the importance of this task in organizing and retrieving information efficiently. We illustrated the process of creating a chatbot capable of handling user queries, showcasing its potential to enhance customer support and user engagement. Further, we delved into building a system that can translate text from one language to another, emphasizing the complexities and advancements in language translation. Finally, we explained how to develop a model that can answer questions based on a given context, a critical component of intelligent systems like virtual assistants.

By combining theoretical knowledge with practical examples, this chapter aimed to provide a comprehensive understanding of how to implement NLP applications using PyTorch. The techniques and methodologies discussed here are foundational for anyone looking to harness the power of NLP in real-world scenarios. As you continue your journey in NLP, these examples serve as a springboard for exploring more advanced models and applications, pushing the boundaries of what machines can understand and accomplish through natural language. In the next chapter, we will discuss the future trends in NLP. We will also discuss the advances in pre-trained language models, multilingual NLP, cross-lingual transfer learning, explainable AI in NLP, the integration of NLP with computer vision, and reinforcement learning for NLP.

Points to Remember

- Tokenization is splitting text into individual words or tokens.
- Accuracy measures the proportion of correct predictions.

- F1 Score considers both precision and recall, providing a balanced measure of model performance.
- Exact Match (EM) measures the proportion of predictions that exactly match the true answers, used in QA systems.
- Sentiment Analysis is a technique that involves classifying text into sentiment categories such as positive, negative, or neutral.
- Text Classification is essential for organizing and retrieving information efficiently. It involves categorizing text into predefined topics or classes.
- Question Answering Systems utilize transformer models such as BERT for understanding and responding to queries.

Multiple Choice Questions

1. What is the primary goal of Sentiment Analysis?
   a. To generate new text based on given prompts
   b. To classify text into sentiment categories such as positive, negative, or neutral
   c. To translate text from one language to another
   d. To categorize text into predefined topics or classes
2. Which model architecture is commonly used for machine translation tasks?
   a. Convolutional Neural Networks (CNNs)
   b. Recurrent Neural Networks (RNNs)
   c. Sequence-to-Sequence (Seq2Seq) models
   d. Generative Adversarial Networks (GANs)
3. What is the purpose of an attention mechanism in Seq2Seq models?
   a. To reduce the number of parameters in the model
   b. To focus on relevant parts of the input sequence
   c. To increase the training speed
   d. To generate random noise for data augmentation
4. Which optimizer is widely used for its efficiency and adaptability in training NLP models?
   a. SGD
   b. Adam

c. RMSprop

d. Adagrad

5. What does the Exact Match (EM) metric measure in Question Answering systems?

   a. The proportion of predictions that partially match the true answers

   b. The proportion of predictions that exactly match the true answers

   c. The average length of predicted answers

   d. The computational efficiency of the model

6. Which of the following is NOT a step in data preprocessing for NLP tasks?

   a. Tokenization

   b. Removing stop words

   c. Training the model

   d. Converting text to numerical representations

7. What is the main advantage of using transformer models such as BERT in NLP tasks?

   a. They are faster to train than traditional models

   b. They can capture complex language patterns and context

   c. They require less data for training

   d. They are easier to implement than Seq2Seq models

8. In Chatbot Development, what is the role of the decoder in a Seq2Seq model?

   a. To process the input sequence and generate a context vector

   b. To generate the target sequence using the context vector

   c. To tokenize the input sequence

   d. To evaluate the model's performance

9. Which evaluation metric considers both precision and recall, providing a balanced measure of model performance?

   a. Accuracy

   b. F1 Score

   c. Exact Match (EM)
   d. Perplexity
10. What is the primary task of a Question Answering system?
   a. To translate questions into multiple languages
   b. To answer questions based on a given context
   c. To classify questions into different categories
   d. To generate new questions based on a given context

Answers

1. b
2. c
3. b
4. b
5. b
6. c
7. b
8. b
9. b
10. b

Questions

1. Explain the process of data preprocessing in NLP tasks and why it is important.
2. Describe the architecture of a Sequence-to-Sequence (Seq2Seq) model and its applications in NLP.
3. Discuss the role and importance of attention mechanisms in Seq2Seq models.
4. How does a transformer model such as BERT differ from traditional RNN-based models in handling NLP tasks?
5. What are the key steps involved in training a Sentiment Analysis model using PyTorch?

6. Illustrate the process of building a Text Classification model for news articles, including data preprocessing, model selection, and evaluation.
7. Explain the components and workflow of a Chatbot developed using PyTorch. How does it process user inputs and generate responses?
8. Discuss the challenges and solutions associated with Neural Machine Translation. How do Seq2Seq models with attention mechanisms address these challenges?
9. Describe the evaluation metrics used for Question Answering systems and their significance in measuring model performance.
10. How can the techniques and models discussed in this chapter be extended or adapted to other NLP tasks? Provide examples of potential applications.

Key Terms

- **Natural Language Processing (NLP)**: A field of artificial intelligence that focuses on the interaction between computers and humans through natural language.
- **PyTorch**: An open-source machine learning library used for applications such as computer vision and natural language processing.
- **Sentiment Analysis**: The process of determining the sentiment or emotional tone behind a series of words, used to understand the attitudes, opinions, and emotions expressed within an online mention.
- **Text Classification**: The task of assigning a set of predefined categories to open-ended text.
- **Chatbot**: A software application used to conduct an online chat conversation via text or text-to-speech, instead of providing direct contact with a live human agent.
- **Neural Machine Translation (NMT)**: A type of machine translation that uses neural network models to translate text from one language to another.
- **Question Answering (QA)**: A computer science discipline within the fields of information retrieval and natural language processing, focused on building systems that automatically answer questions posed by humans.
- **Sequence-to-Sequence (Seq2Seq) Model**: A model that uses two neural networks to transform sequences from one domain to sequences in another domain, commonly used for tasks such as machine translation and chatbot development.

- **Transformer Model**: A type of deep learning model introduced in 2017, designed to handle sequential data by relying entirely on self-attention mechanisms to draw global dependencies between input and output.
- **Bidirectional Encoder Representations from Transformers (BERT)**: A transformer-based model designed to pre-train deep bidirectional representations by jointly conditioning on both left and right context in all layers.
- **Attention Mechanism**: A technique that enables the model to focus on relevant parts of the input sequence when producing each element of the output sequence.
- **Tokenization**: The process of splitting text into individual words or tokens.
- **Pre-Trained Model**: A model that has been previously trained on a large dataset and can be fine-tuned for specific tasks.
- **Adam Optimizer**: An optimization algorithm used for training deep learning models, known for its efficiency and low memory requirements.
- **Cross-Entropy Loss**: A loss function commonly used for classification tasks, measuring the difference between the predicted probability distribution and the true distribution.
- **Exact Match (EM)**: An evaluation metric that measures the proportion of predictions that exactly match the true answers.
- **F1 Score**: A measure of a model's accuracy that considers both the precision and the recall.
- **Token Type IDs**: Input tokens that distinguish between different types of sequences, used in models such as BERT.
- **Context Vector**: In Seq2Seq models, a vector that represents the entire input sequence is used by the decoder to generate the output sequence.
- **Self-Attention**: A mechanism within the transformer model that allows the model to weigh the importance of different words in a sentence, considering their context when processing each word.

CHAPTER 10
Future Trends in Natural Language Processing and PyTorch

Introduction

There have been a lot of advancements in the field of Natural Language Processing (NLP) in recent years. The rapid advancements in the field of NLP are due to the evolution of machine learning techniques and the widespread use of deep learning frameworks. As NLP evolves, there have been major developments in how machines understand and generate human language, powering applications ranging from conversational agents to real-time translation and sentiment analysis.

In this chapter, we will delve into future trends in NLP that lead to significant opportunities and innovation in the field of language generation and understanding.

We will explore advances in Pre-trained Language Models, which have revolutionized the ability of models to generalize across diverse tasks and domains. This chapter also discusses Multilingual NLP and Cross-Lingual Transfer Learning, focusing on how models are being adapted to handle multiple languages and dialects with fewer resources. These techniques are expanding the reach of NLP to regions where labeled data is scarce or languages are underrepresented. This chapter also delves into Explainable AI in NLP, addressing the growing need for transparency in AI models. It discusses the integration of NLP with Computer Vision, an interdisciplinary trend that seeks to bridge the gap between language and visual information. Additionally, this chapter delves into Reinforcement Learning for NLP, an approach that has led to the advent of new possibilities for training models that interact with dynamic environments, learn from feedback, and improve iteratively.

Structure

In this chapter, we will discuss the following topics:

- Advances in Pre-Trained Language Models
- Multilingual NLP and Cross-Lingual Transfer Learning
- Explainable AI in NLP
- Integration of NLP with Computer Vision
- Reinforcement Learning for NLP

Advances in Pre-Trained Language Models

Pre-trained language models have resulted in the evolution of natural language processing (NLP) by serving as foundational models that can be fine-tuned for specific tasks. These advances have made it easier to solve a wide range of NLP tasks with high performance and efficiency. Recent developments have focused on scaling models, enhancing their understanding, and expanding their capabilities across multiple domains and languages. The advances in Pre-trained Language Models can be seen in the following ways:

- **Scaling Up Pre-Trained Models**: One of the most noticeable trends in pre-trained language models is their increasing size.

  These larger models, consisting of billions and even trillions of parameters, can capture deeper linguistic and contextual nuances, resulting in remarkable performance across multiple NLP tasks.

  As models grow larger, their capacity to understand more complex patterns and relationships improves. This scaling has led to improvements in tasks such as text generation, machine translation, and question-answering.

  However, increasing model size also brings challenges such as computational costs, memory constraints, and the need for efficient hardware support. PyTorch, with its flexibility and support for distributed training, is increasingly being used to train and fine-tune these models on large-scale datasets.

- **Architectural Innovations**: While scaling model size has led to significant improvements, architectural innovations have also played a major role in advancing pre-trained language models. Models are no longer just about increasing parameters; new architectures have improved their efficiency and performance.

- **Sparse and Efficient Transformers**: One limitation of traditional transformer models is their quadratic complexity in relation to input length. To address this, newer models such as Longformer and BigBird introduce sparse attention mechanisms that enable the processing of longer sequences with fewer computational resources.

- **Self-Supervised Learning and Unsupervised Pre-training**: The shift from supervised learning to self-supervised learning has been a critical advance in the development of pre-trained language models. In self-supervised learning, models are trained on vast amounts of text data without the need for manually labeled datasets. This unsupervised pre-training phase is followed by fine-tuning specific downstream tasks.
- **Masked Language Modeling**: Models such as BERT introduced the concept of masked language modeling, where parts of the input are masked, and the model learns to predict the missing words. This helps the model develop a deep understanding of context and linguistic structure.
- **Zero-shot, Few-shot, and Prompt-based Learning**: A major advancement in pre-trained language models is the ability to perform zero-shot and few-shot learning, where models can generalize to new tasks with little or no task-specific training. Tasks such as Translation or Question Answering are performed using it.
- **Ethics, Bias, and Responsible AI**: As pre-trained models grow in size and power, concerns about their ethical use and biases embedded in training data have become more prominent. The issues related to data bias, fairness, and interpretability may become increasingly important. Pre-trained models reflect biases present in the data they are trained on. This includes biases related to race, gender, and socioeconomic status. Researchers are now focusing on ways to mitigate these biases, such as through adversarial training or data augmentation techniques. The power of pre-trained models brings a responsibility to use them ethically, ensuring they do not reinforce harmful stereotypes or produce misinformation.

Multilingual NLP and Cross-lingual Transfer Learning

In today's world, where NLP is advancing, there are numerous applications of NLP. NLP applications may involve processing and understanding multiple languages.

Multilingual NLP and cross-lingual transfer learning enable models to work across different languages, thereby broadening the reach and applicability of NLP solutions.

Importance of Multilingual NLP

Multilingual NLP is critical for several reasons:

- **Global Accessibility**: By supporting multiple languages, NLP applications can facilitate a broader audience, ensuring inclusivity and accessibility for users worldwide.

- **Data Efficiency**: Leveraging knowledge from high-resource languages to improve performance in low-resource languages reduces the need for extensive language-specific data.
- **Cultural Relevance**: Multilingual models can capture cultural context, which enhances the relevance and accuracy of NLP applications in different regions.
- **Business Expansion**: Companies can expand their market reach and provide better customer service by offering multilingual support in their products and services.

Challenges in Multilingual NLP

Despite its advantages, multilingual NLP presents several challenges:

- **Data Scarcity**: Many languages lack large, high-quality annotated datasets, making it difficult to train effective models.
- **Language Diversity**: Languages differ in syntax, morphology, and semantics, requiring models to adapt to these variations.
- **Resource Constraints**: Training multilingual models can be computationally expensive, requiring significant resources for processing large datasets in multiple languages.
- **Evaluation Complexity**: Evaluating multilingual models is challenging due to the lack of standardized benchmarks across languages.

Techniques for Multilingual NLP

Several techniques are used to address the challenges of multilingual NLP:

- **Pre-Trained Multilingual Models**: Models such as Multilingual BERT (mBERT) and Cross-lingual Language Model-RoBERTa (XLM-R) are pre-trained on large corpora of multiple languages, capturing cross-lingual representations that can be fine-tuned for specific tasks.
- **Shared Vocabulary and Embeddings**: Using a shared vocabulary and embedding space for multiple languages allows models to learn common features and relationships across languages.
- **Joint Training**: Training a single model on data from multiple languages simultaneously encourages the model to learn cross-lingual patterns and representations.
- **Transfer Learning**: Fine-tuning a model pre-trained on a high-resource language for a low-resource language can improve performance by transferring knowledge from the source language.

Cross-Lingual Transfer Learning

Cross-lingual transfer learning is a powerful approach that leverages knowledge from one language to improve performance in another. This involves several steps:

- **Pre-Training**: Train a model on a large, multilingual corpus to learn language-agnostic features and representations.
- **Fine-Tuning**: Fine-tune the pre-trained model on a specific task using data from the target language, transferring knowledge from the source languages.
- **Zero-Shot Learning**: In some cases, models can perform tasks in a new language without any fine-tuning, based on the cross-lingual representations learned during pre-training.

Building Multilingual Models with PyTorch

PyTorch is used for building and training multilingual models. Consider the following simplified example of using a pre-trained multilingual model for text classification:

```
import torch
from transformers import XLMRobertaForSequenceClassification,
XLMRobertaTokenizer

# Load pre-trained model and tokenizer
model_name = 'xlm-roberta-base'
model = XLMRobertaForSequenceClassification.from_pretrained(model_name,
num_labels=2)
tokenizer = XLMRobertaTokenizer.from_pretrained(model_name)

# Sample multilingual data
texts = ["Hello, how are you?", "Hola, ¿cómo estás?", "Bonjour, comment
ça va?"]
labels = [0, 0, 0]  # Example labels

# Tokenize and encode texts
inputs = tokenizer(texts, padding=True, truncation=True, return_
tensors='pt')

# Forward pass
outputs = model(**inputs)
logits = outputs.logits

# Loss and optimizer
criterion = torch.nn.CrossEntropyLoss()
optimizer = torch.optim.Adam(model.parameters(), lr=1e-5)
```

```
# Example training loop
for epoch in range(3):
    model.train()
    optimizer.zero_grad()
    outputs = model(**inputs)
    loss = criterion(outputs.logits, torch.tensor(labels))
    loss.backward()
    optimizer.step()
    print(f'Epoch {epoch + 1}, Loss: {loss.item()}')

# Model evaluation
model.eval()
with torch.no_grad():
    outputs = model(**inputs)
    predictions = torch.argmax(outputs.logits, dim=1)
    print(predictions)
```

In this example, we use XLM-R, a pre-trained multilingual model from the Hugging Face Transformers library, for a simple text classification task.

Explainable AI in NLP

As NLP models become more complex and pervasive in critical applications, understanding how these models make decisions has become increasingly important. Explainable AI (XAI) aims to make the decision-making processes of AI systems transparent, interpretable, and understandable to humans. This is especially crucial in NLP, where models are often used in critical applications such as healthcare, finance, and legal systems.

Explainable AI in NLP is essential for the following reasons:

- **Trust and Transparency**: Users are more likely to trust and adopt NLP models if they can understand how the models arrive at their conclusions. Transparency helps build confidence in AI systems.
- **Ethical and Legal Compliance**: In certain domains, regulatory requirements mandate that AI decisions be explainable. For example, the GDPR in Europe includes the "right to explanation" for automated decisions.
- **Error Analysis and Debugging**: Explainable models allow developers to identify and rectify errors more effectively, improving the overall performance and reliability of the system.
- **Bias Detection and Mitigation**: Understanding model decisions helps identify and mitigate biases, ensuring fair and equitable outcomes for all users.

Techniques for Explainable AI in NLP

Several techniques are employed to enhance the explainability of NLP models. These include:

- **Feature Importance**: Identifying which features (words or phrases) are most influential in a model's decision can provide insights into its reasoning process. Techniques such as attention mechanisms and SHapley Additive exPlanations (SHAP) are commonly used.
- **Attention Mechanisms**: Attention mechanisms in models such as Transformers highlight which parts of the input text the model focuses on when making a decision, providing a form of interpretability.
- **Saliency Maps**: Saliency maps visualize the contribution of each input token to the model's output, helping to identify which parts of the text are most relevant to the prediction.

Integration of NLP with Computer Vision

The integration of Natural Language Processing (NLP) with Computer Vision (CV) has led to groundbreaking advancements in artificial intelligence, enabling machines to understand and interpret multimodal data that combines text and images. This convergence allows for the development of sophisticated applications such as image captioning, visual question answering, and multimodal sentiment analysis. In this section, we will explore the significance of integrating NLP with CV, the techniques involved, and how PyTorch can be utilized to build these integrated models.

Importance of Integrating NLP with CV

The integration of NLP with CV is crucial for several reasons:

- **Enhanced Understanding**: Combining text and visual information allows models to gain a more comprehensive understanding of the content, leading to more accurate and context-aware predictions.
- **Improved User Interaction**: Applications such as chatbots and virtual assistants can provide more intuitive and interactive experiences by understanding and responding to both text and images.
- **Rich Content Analysis**: Analyzing multimodal data enables deeper insights in areas such as social media analysis, where users frequently post images with accompanying text.
- **Innovative Applications**: The synergy between NLP and CV drives innovation in various domains, including healthcare (medical image analysis with textual

reports), education (interactive learning tools), and entertainment (enhanced content recommendation systems).

Techniques for Integrating NLP with CV

Several techniques are used to integrate NLP with CV effectively:

- **Joint Embedding Spaces**: Creating a common embedding space for both text and images allows models to learn shared representations, facilitating the fusion of multimodal data.
- **Attention Mechanisms**: Attention mechanisms help models focus on relevant parts of the text and image, improving the interpretability and performance of multimodal tasks.
- **Multimodal Transformers**: Transformer architectures, originally designed for NLP, have been extended to handle multimodal data, allowing for more sophisticated interactions between text and images.
- **Cross-Modal Transfer Learning**: Leveraging pre-trained models from one modality (for example, vision) to enhance performance in another modality (for example, text) through transfer learning.
- **Fusion Techniques**: Combining features from both modalities using techniques such as concatenation, element-wise addition, or more complex fusion methods to enable joint processing.

Reinforcement Learning for NLP

Reinforcement Learning (RL) has gained significant attention in the field of Natural Language Processing (NLP) due to its potential to optimize complex decision-making tasks. Unlike traditional supervised learning, which relies on labeled datasets, RL focuses on learning policies that maximize cumulative rewards through interaction with an environment. This section explores the significance of RL in NLP, key RL concepts, common applications, and how PyTorch can be used to implement RL-based NLP models.

Importance of Reinforcement Learning in NLP

Reinforcement Learning is crucial in NLP for several reasons:

- **Dynamic Decision Making**: RL is well-suited for tasks that involve sequential decision-making, such as dialogue systems and text generation, where the model's decisions at each step influence future outcomes.

- **Exploration and Exploitation**: RL enables models to explore various strategies and learn optimal policies by balancing exploration (trying new actions) and exploitation (using known actions).
- **Handling Sparse Rewards**: RL can be effective in scenarios with sparse or delayed rewards, such as long-term language tasks, where the immediate reward might not be apparent.
- **Adaptation and Personalization**: RL allows models to adapt and personalize interactions based on user feedback, improving the overall user experience.

Key Concepts in Reinforcement Learning

- **Agent and Environment**: The agent interacts with the environment by taking actions and receiving rewards. The goal is to learn a policy that maximizes the cumulative reward.
- **State and Action**: The state represents the current situation, while the action is the decision made by the agent. The policy maps states to actions.
- **Reward and Cumulative Reward**: The reward is the feedback received after taking an action. The cumulative reward is the total reward accumulated over time.
- **Policy and Value Function**: The policy defines the agent's behavior, while the value function estimates the expected cumulative reward for a given state or state-action pair.

Common Applications of RL in NLP

- **Dialogue Systems**: RL is used to train conversational agents that can generate coherent and contextually appropriate responses by optimizing long-term user satisfaction.
- **Text Generation**: RL helps improve the quality of generated text by optimizing metrics such as fluency, coherence, and diversity, often using rewards based on human feedback or automatic evaluation metrics.
- **Machine Translation**: RL can enhance translation quality by directly optimizing translation metrics such as BLEU or human judgment scores.
- **Information Retrieval**: RL-based models can learn to rank documents or responses by maximizing user engagement and satisfaction.
- **Text Summarization**: RL allows models to generate concise and informative summaries by optimizing relevance and readability metrics.

Implementing RL-Based NLP Models with PyTorch

PyTorch provides a flexible and powerful framework for implementing RL algorithms. Here is an example of using RL for a text generation task:

```
import torch
import torch.nn as nn
import torch.optim as optim
import numpy as np

# Define the RNN-based language model
class RNNLanguageModel(nn.Module):
    def __init__(self, vocab_size, embed_size, hidden_size):
        super(RNNLanguageModel, self).__init__()
        self.embedding = nn.Embedding(vocab_size, embed_size)
        self.rnn = nn.LSTM(embed_size, hidden_size, batch_first=True)
        self.fc = nn.Linear(hidden_size, vocab_size)

    def forward(self, x, hidden):
        x = self.embedding(x)
        out, hidden = self.rnn(x, hidden)
        out = self.fc(out)
        return out, hidden

    def init_hidden(self, batch_size):
        return (torch.zeros(1, batch_size, hidden_size),
                torch.zeros(1, batch_size, hidden_size))

# Define the reward function
def reward_function(output, target):
    reward = np.sum(output == target) / len(target)  # Example reward:
proportion of correct predictions
    return reward

# Training parameters
vocab_size = 5000
embed_size = 128
hidden_size = 256
learning_rate = 0.01
num_epochs = 10
batch_size = 64

# Initialize model, loss function, and optimizer
model = RNNLanguageModel(vocab_size, embed_size, hidden_size)
criterion = nn.CrossEntropyLoss()
optimizer = optim.Adam(model.parameters(), lr=learning_rate)
```

```
# Training loop with RL
for epoch in range(num_epochs):
    model.train()
    total_loss = 0
    total_reward = 0

    for batch in data_loader:  # Assume data_loader is defined and pro-
vides batches of (input, target)
        input, target = batch
        hidden = model.init_hidden(batch_size)
        optimizer.zero_grad()

        output, hidden = model(input, hidden)
        loss = criterion(output.view(-1, vocab_size), target.view(-1))
        loss.backward()
        optimizer.step()

        total_loss += loss.item()

        # Calculate reward
        reward = reward_function(torch.argmax(output, dim=-1), target)
        total_reward += reward

    print(f'Epoch {epoch + 1}, Loss: {total_loss / len(data_loader)},
Reward: {total_reward / len(data_loader)}')
```

In this example, we define an RNN-based language model for text generation. The model is trained using a reward function that encourages the generation of correct predictions. The training loop updates the model parameters to maximize the reward, showcasing a simple form of RL for NLP.

Reinforcement Learning offers a powerful framework for optimizing complex, sequential decision-making tasks in NLP. By leveraging RL, models can dynamically learn from their interactions with the environment, improving their performance in tasks such as dialogue systems, text generation, machine translation, information retrieval, and text summarization. PyTorch provides the necessary tools and flexibility to implement RL algorithms, enabling the development of advanced RL-based NLP models. As the field continues to evolve, the integration of RL in NLP will play a crucial role in pushing the boundaries of what AI can achieve in understanding and generating human language.

Conclusion

The future of Natural Language Processing (NLP) is rich with possibilities, fueled by continuous innovation in both machine learning techniques and the tools that support them, such as PyTorch. This chapter explored some of the most promising trends shaping the future of NLP, each presenting new opportunities to enhance how machines understand and interact with human language. Advances in pre-trained language models have significantly elevated the capabilities of NLP systems, making them more versatile, accurate, and capable of handling complex language tasks with minimal supervision.

These models, with their scalability and ability to generalize, have become the backbone of many modern NLP applications. The rise of multilingual NLP and cross-lingual transfer learning is opening up new possibilities for global communication, breaking down language barriers, and democratizing access to NLP technologies for underrepresented languages. This trend is vital for making NLP more inclusive and impactful on a global scale. Explainable AI in NLP is increasingly important as AI systems take on more critical roles in decision-making processes. Ensuring that these systems are transparent, interpretable, and trustworthy will be essential to fostering trust in NLP applications, especially in sensitive domains such as healthcare, finance, and law. The integration of NLP with computer vision represents a new frontier in AI, where the convergence of language and visual information enables richer and more nuanced understanding. This trend is already transforming tasks such as image captioning, visual question answering, and multimodal learning.

Lastly, reinforcement learning in NLP is paving the way for more adaptive, interactive, and intelligent language models that can improve over time through feedback. This approach is key for developing advanced conversational agents, task-oriented systems, and other applications requiring dynamic decision-making. Together, these trends reflect a future where NLP is more powerful, flexible, and integrated into our daily lives. PyTorch will continue to play a crucial role in enabling researchers and developers to push the boundaries of NLP, offering the tools and flexibility needed to experiment, innovate, and build the next generation of language models.

Points to Remember

- Advances in Pre-trained Language Models: Pre-trained models have revolutionized NLP by allowing models to generalize across tasks with minimal fine-tuning.
- Increasing model size and architectural innovations (for example, sparse transformers) have led to major advancements in the field of NLP.
- Multilingual NLP and Cross-Lingual Transfer Learning: Multilingual models enable NLP systems to handle multiple languages without extensive retraining for each language.
- Cross-lingual transfer learning allows models to leverage knowledge from high-resource languages to low-resource languages, improving accessibility.
- PyTorch supports multilingual training pipelines and cross-lingual fine-tuning techniques.

- Explainable AI in NLP: Explainable AI focuses on making NLP models more transparent, interpretable, and accountable for their decisions. Explainability is crucial in sensitive applications such as healthcare, finance, and legal domains, where understanding model decisions is essential.
- Integration of NLP with Computer Vision: NLP and computer vision are being combined to enable models to process both text and visual data, leading to applications such as image captioning and visual question answering.
- Multimodal models leverage both text and image inputs to create richer, more comprehensive AI systems.
- Reinforcement Learning (RL) allows NLP models to learn through interaction and feedback, leading to more adaptive and responsive systems.
- PyTorch implements reinforcement learning algorithms through libraries such as TorchRL.
- Pre-trained models must be used responsibly, as they can inadvertently reinforce societal biases present in training data.
- Ethical considerations, such as fairness, accountability, and transparency, are increasingly becoming integral to NLP development.

Multiple Choice Questions

1. What is the primary advantage of using pre-trained language models in NLP?
   a. They require no training at all
   b. They can generalize across tasks with minimal fine-tuning
   c. They are faster than rule-based systems
   d. They work only with structured data
2. Which of the following is an example of a multilingual NLP model?
   a. GPT-3
   b. BERT
   c. mBERT
   d. RoBERTa
3. Explainable AI in NLP is crucial because:
   a. It helps make models faster
   b. It ensures that models provide entertainment
   c. It makes models more transparent and interpretable
   d. It reduces the need for data

4. What is the main goal of cross-lingual transfer learning in NLP?
   a. To translate text between two languages
   b. To improve model performance on low-resource languages using knowledge from high-resource languages
   c. To process images and videos in different languages
   d. To develop voice assistants
5. The integration of NLP with computer vision enables tasks such as:
   a. Sentiment analysis
   b. Named entity recognition
   c. Image captioning
   d. Grammar correction
6. What role does reinforcement learning play in NLP?
   a. It helps models learn from static datasets
   b. It trains models to learn from feedback and interaction
   c. It improves the speed of training language models
   d. It ensures that models are interpretable
7. Which PyTorch library is commonly used for computer vision tasks in combination with NLP?
   a. TorchVision
   b. Transformers
   c. TorchText
   d. SciPy
8. What is a key challenge for Explainable AI in NLP?
   a. Making models train faster
   b. Ensuring models can be deployed in multiple languages
   c. Developing methods to explain complex model decisions
   d. Training models on structured data

9. How does reinforcement learning improve the performance of conversational agents?
    a. By feeding static data to the agents
    b. By allowing agents to adapt through feedback and rewards
    c. By making agents faster at processing text
    d. By improving the data storage capability
10. Why is the PyTorch framework preferred for developing cutting-edge NLP models?
    a. It requires less computational power
    b. It offers flexibility and dynamic computation graphs, making experimentation easier
    c. It only works with small datasets
    d. It does not support deep learning tasks

Answers

1. b
2. c
3. c
4. b
5. c
6. b
7. a
8. c
9. b
10. b

Questions

1. Explain how pre-trained language models have transformed the field of NLP and discuss their advantages over traditional NLP methods.

2. Describe the concept of multilingual NLP and explain how cross-lingual transfer learning helps overcome the challenges of low-resource languages.
3. Discuss the importance of Explainable AI in NLP. How does it contribute to building trust in AI systems, particularly in critical domains such as healthcare and finance?
4. How does the integration of NLP with computer vision contribute to advancements in tasks such as image captioning and visual question answering? Provide examples of real-world applications.
5. Explain the role of reinforcement learning in NLP. How does it differ from traditional supervised learning methods in developing conversational agents or task-oriented systems?
6. What are the key challenges and ethical considerations in deploying large-scale pre-trained language models in real-world applications?
7. What are some of the limitations of current pre-trained language models? Suggest possible future directions or improvements that could address these limitations.
8. How do you foresee the future of NLP evolving with trends such as multilingualism, multimodal learning, and reinforcement learning? Discuss how these trends might shape future applications of language technologies.

Key Terms

- **Pre-Trained Language Models**: Models that are trained on large corpora of text before being fine-tuned on specific tasks. This enables them to generalize across multiple NLP tasks with minimal additional training.
- **Transfer Learning**: A machine learning technique where a model trained on one task is repurposed for a different, but related, task, often with better performance and reduced training time.
- **Multilingual NLP**: The ability of NLP models to process, understand, and generate text in multiple languages, often with the help of multilingual training data or shared model architectures.
- **Cross-Lingual Transfer Learning**: A method that leverages knowledge from high-resource languages to improve the performance of models in low-resource languages, reducing the need for large amounts of labeled data.
- **Explainable AI (XAI)**: A branch of AI focused on making machine learning models more transparent and interpretable, especially in decision-making processes, to ensure trust and accountability.
- **Multimodal Learning**: An approach where models are designed to process

and integrate data from multiple modalities, such as text, images, and audio, to perform tasks such as image captioning and visual question answering.

- **Reinforcement Learning (RL)**: A learning paradigm where agents learn to make decisions by interacting with the environment and receiving feedback in the form of rewards or penalties. This type of learning is commonly used in dynamic and interactive systems.
- **Bidirectional Encoder Representations from Transformers (BERT)**: It is a transformer-based model that processes text bi-directionally. This model considers the context from both the left and right of a word to understand its meaning.
- **Generative Pre-Trained Transformer (GPT)**: A family of transformer-based language models that generate human-like text by predicting the next word in a sequence. It is, widely used in text generation and conversational agents.
- **Multilingual BERT (mBERT)**: A version of BERT that is trained on data from multiple languages, allowing it to handle text in different languages and perform cross-lingual tasks.
- **Attention Mechanism**: A technique used in transformer models to focus on specific parts of the input sequence when making predictions, allowing models to capture dependencies between distant words in text.
- **Transformer Architecture**: A deep learning architecture based on self-attention mechanisms that have become the backbone of most modern NLP models, including BERT and GPT.
- **Natural Language Processing (NLP)**: A field of artificial intelligence that enables machines to understand, interpret, and generate human language.
- **Fine Tuning**: The process of taking a pre-trained model and adapting it to a specific task or dataset by further training on that task with a smaller amount of data.

Index

M

N

T

W